NEW POEMS

1961

A P.E.N. Anthology of
Contemporary Poetry

Edited by

WILLIAM PLOMER
ANTHONY THWAITE
HILARY CORKE

D1481608

HUTCHINSON OF LONDON

HUTCHINSON & CO. (*Publishers*) LTD
178–202 Great Portland Street, London, W.1

London Melbourne Sydney
Auckland Bombay Toronto
Johannesburg New York

★

First published 1961

*This book has been set in Spectrum type face. It has
been printed in Great Britain by The Anchor Press,
Ltd., in Tiptree, Essex, on Smooth Wove paper and
bound by Taylor Garnett Evans & Co., Ltd., in
Watford, Herts*

ACKNOWLEDGMENTS

Acknowledgments are due to the following publications which have included the poems indicated in their pages:

The Anglo-Welsh Review for the poem by Glyn Jones.

Apollon (Kyoto, Japan) for the poem by James Kirkup.

The Critical Quarterly for the poem by John Holloway.

Encounter for the poems by Kingsley Amis, Michael Hamburger, and Elizabeth Jennings ('One Flesh').

Granta for the poem by Janet Burroway.

The Listener for the poems by Patricia Beer, Graham Hough, Elizabeth Jennings ('The Diamond Cutter'), Francis King, Thomas Kinsella, George MacBeth, Betty Parvin, Jonathan Price, Vernon Scannell ('The Telephone Number'), Stevie Smith, Hal Summers, Donald Thomas, Anthony Thwaite, and John Wain.

The London Magazine for the poems by Charles Causley and Louis MacNeice.

Mademoiselle (*U.S.A.*) for the poem by Jonathan Price.

New Departures for the poem by Adrian Mitchell.

New Statesman for the poem by Edward Lucie-Smith.

The Observer for the poem by Christopher Hampton.

Outposts for the poems by Peter Redgrove and Noël Welch.

The Outsider (*New Orleans*) for the poem by Gael Turnbull.

Poetry and Audience (Leeds University) for the poems by G. W. Ireland and Sydney Tremayne.

The Spectator for the poem by D. J. Enright.

Threshold for the poem by Richard Kell.

The Times Literary Supplement for the poem by William Plomer, the poem by Julian Ennis (*published originally under the pen-name of Noel Scott*) and a poem by Ted Hughes ('Thistles').

Transatlantic Review for the poem by Roy Fuller.

Acknowledgments are also due to the B.B.C. for poems by the following which have been broadcast:

Kingsley Amis, Zoë Bailey, Patricia Beer, Thomas Blackburn, Janet Burroway, R. N. Currey, Clifford Dyment, Christopher Hampton, Ted Hughes ('Thistles'), G. W. Ireland, Ada Jackson, Thomas Kinsella, Philip Larkin, Edward Lucie-Smith, George MacBeth, Adrian Mitchell, Jonathan Price, Vernon Scannell ('Personal Interview' and 'The Telephone Number'), E. J. Scovell, and John Wain.

Permission to reprint or broadcast any poems in this anthology must be obtained from Hutchinson & Co. (Publishers) Ltd., 178–202 Great Portland Street, London, W.1. The usual acknowledgement must be made to the publishers and to *New Poems—1961,* the ninth in the P.E.N. series of annual anthologies of contemporary poetry. Letters to contributors will be forwarded if addressed to International P.E.N., 62–63 Glebe Place, Chelsea, London, S.W.3.

CONTENTS

INTRODUCTION BY THE EDITORS

When three editors work together to prepare an anthology total unanimity cannot be expected. We have found ourselves mostly in agreement about the virtues or weaknesses of the many poems submitted to us; but in a remaining minority of cases inclusions and rejections have been made in the face of sturdy opposition. In making concessions to one another we have acknowledged that our own inclinations towards or away from some poet or poem could be overridden; in advocating, perhaps alone, some inclusion each of us has indulged in hard bargaining.

We do not claim that we have been able to include examples of the work of all good poets now writing in England; the absence, in particular, of some older, well-known, and justly admired poets does not imply disregard on our part. We do claim to have brought together characteristic poems by poets already known and poems of varying distinction by others less well known or with names new to us. And we are glad to have been able to include three longish poems of quite different kinds.

We have noticed that in the constant tug-of-cold-war in the world today many poets have been moved to write by the open or implied threat of long-distance genocide, and that this natural impulse does not necessarily, or even generally, lead to very satisfactory verse. Other poets, not looking far beyond their own noses, are occupied with notably domestic themes. Readers who believe love of what is known to be as proper a subject for poetry as fear of the unknown would have reason to complain only if the treatment of any chosen theme were found to be marred by too little exercise of intellect and imagination or by technical inadequacy.

We wish to thank Miss Helen Rogers for her valuable help in the processes of preparing the book for the printer.

W.P.

H.T.C.

A.S.T.

NEW POEMS

1961

Kingsley Amis

SIGHT UNSEEN

As I was waiting for the bus
    A girl came up the street,
Detectable as double-plus
    At seven hundred feet.

Her head was high, her step was free,
    Her face a lyric blur;
Her waist was narrow, I could see,
    But not the rest of her.

At fifty feet I watched her stop,
    Bite at a glove, then veer
Aside into some pointless shop,
    Never to reappear.

This happens every bloody day:
    They about-turn, they duck
Into their car and drive away,
    They hide behind a truck.

Look, if they knew me—understood,
    There might be cause to run;
Or if they saw me, well and good;
    And yet they don't, not one.

Love at first sight—by this we mean
    A stellar entrant thrown
Clear on the psyche's radar-screen,
    Recognized before known.

All right: things work the opposite
    Way with the poles reversed;
It's galling, though, when girls omit
    To switch the set on first.

Zoë Bailey

CALYPTORHYNCHUS FUNEREUS
(*Funereal Cockatoo*)

One wan bird walks close to the mesh of the aviary,
As though taking pleasure
In my company.

On perches behind him brilliant birds balance and flicker
To preen each flamboyant,
Erratic feather.

Clumsily this bird walks near my prohibited hand.
Draggles one cloudy wing
To stand

Rebuking endearments with a hoarse, broken cry.
I probe for a cause
The inert depths of his eye.

Nothing but light reflected: no sign of pain nor fear.
One horny yellow claw
Grips the upright bar.

But as though tear-weighted, his eyelid falls, downcast.
Despairingly a feather
Drifts to the dust.

Without words I can do nothing he wants me to do.
Useless, I stroke his claw
Unwilling to go.

He cries out desperately, as though for release
From where he is blackly trapped
In a feathered hearse.

His hieroglyph my mind cannot resolve, nor read,
Only a finger through the mesh
Can brush his head

To caress the body of his grave incomprehension
With amity, with amity,
Again and again.

Patricia Beer

DEATH OF A NUN

Here lies Mother Agnes, nun
Who died last night, eighty years old.
Standing beside her, all I see
Is that her flesh has turned to gold.
Not even the tawny parlour blinds
Could make my skin as rich as hers.
Her roots of dying must have sucked
The yellowness of clay and stars.

In former days the holy man
Went up the mountain we are told,
Drew back out of the scorching light
And could not see his God for gold.
It seems as though this nun has stepped
Into the lightning of her death
And captured what she always had,
Contained it, brought it down to earth.

There is no kindness in her face
Nor love, but then there never was.
Love is a symbol, does not need
To see its features in the glass.
Her charity was pure. It lay,
Is lying still, along the bone,
No firmer now her heart is stiff
And metal stands in every vein.

Her name was buried when she took
Her vows, as if her life of prayer
Was uttered from the nerves and cells
Of one who was not really there.
No more impersonal now dead,

No more anonymous and cold,
She is transformed to precious stuff
That bears a general name, like gold.

It should not come as a surprise
To see the beads that she has clutched
Lying across a hand as hard
As any limb that Midas touched.
The alchemy of her disease
Has worked a long-maturing spell
And turned her into gold, yet made
No change in anything at all.

Thomas Blackburn

EPITAPH

By much speaking I fled from silence,
To many friends from the one stranger,
By food and drink I cheated hunger,
And by meek words, abuse and violence.

My loss increased as I grew richer,
My load more great, with lighter burden,
With less guilt, more sought I pardon.
As light flowered I grew blinder.

I quenched my thirst by lack of water,
And found myself where I was absent,
Faith half I proved by the inconstant
Moon: truth because I was a liar.

Now far still from the heart's centre,
But with less storm, less crying,
I wait for birth again, now dying
Has opened its door and let me enter.

THE SCIENTIST
(*For Bob*)

'There's nothing mysterious about the skull.'
He may have been suspicious of my request,
That being mainly a poet, I mainly guessed
There might be an esoteric chance to cull

Some succulent, unfamiliar word; that being
Mainly a woman, I now for his sake embraced
An object I held in fact in some distaste.
But he complied, his slender fingers freeing

(There must be a surgeon somewhere with stubby hands)
The latch that held a coil across 'The suture
Between the parietals and occipital feature.'
And gently, his flesh on the bone disturbed the bands

Which illustrated the way that 'The mandible
Articulates with the temple next to the ear.
The nasal bone gives onto the maxilla here.'
He laughed, 'It's a bore, but it's not expendable;

'The features depend, if not for their shape, on the narrow
Cranium, formed of the commonest elements;
Weighing nine ounces, worth about fourteen cents;
Not even room for what you would call a marrow.'

In words resembling these, he judged them dull:
The specimen, his detail, and my suggestion.
'The skin and the brain, of course, are another question,'
He said again, 'But there's nothing to the skull.'

And that must be so. The quick mind most demands a
Miracle in the covering or the core;
What lies between is shallow and functional fare:
My hand between this thought and the posturing stanza.

But his face belied us both. As he spoke his own
Eyes rhymed depth from the sockets of that example;
His jawline articulated with the temple
Over the words, and his fingers along the bone

Revealed his god in the praying of their plying.
So that, wonderfully, I justify his doubt;
Am moved, as woman to love, as poet to write,
By the mystery and the function of his denying.

GRAVE BY THE SEA

By the crunching, Cornish sea
Walk the man and walk the lover
Innocent as fish that fare
In the high and hooking air
And their deaths discover.

Beneath, you said, this turning tree,
With granite eye and stare of sand
His heart as candid as the clay
A seaman from the stropping bay
Took to the land.

Once this calmed, crystal hand was free
And rang the changes of the heart:
Love, like his life, a world wherein
The white-worm sin wandered not in.
Death played no part.

Wreathed, and with ringing fingers he
Passed like a prince upon the day
And from its four and twenty towers
Shot with his shaft the haggard hours,
Hauled them away.

So he set from the shaken quay
His foot upon the ocean floor
And from the wanting water's teeth
The ice-faced gods above, beneath,
Spat him ashore.

Now in the speaking of the sea
He waits under this written stone,
And kneeling at his freezing frame
I scrub my eye to see his name

And read my own.

MIGRATION

Salmon that climb the stream
  the prodigal fish come home
from courses they have swum
  and at the salmon-gate
each silver younger son
  still knows the latch of the river
where once he swam from spat.

The fish that climbs the fall
  goes back where he began;
I no less punctual
  over the weir of woman
swim for my origin—
  glad that the trip's not fatal
to me as to the salmon.

Hilary Corke

THE EVENING WALK

To bless us now after the dark week
The moon returns, a silver sliver
Chasing the sunset sun:
Out of blue ground, against green sky
(Strange reversal)
The elms rear, the whitebeams'
Cannon-puffs in the yew wood
Are pink with funerals, on rosy edge
The inland gull cuts home; the worm in the clod
Burrows out of darkness into darkness. . . .

Meanwhile in our walled demesne the aproned gardener
With rake and string returns from plotting,
Stacks hoes in shed, the sounds of my children
Bowl in the alley, the sounds of my birds,
Of birdsounds twingling to endusked conclusions
Baffling as Chinese, and the shadows
Are so long now they are no longer.

I will lay out day with the best of you, in the universal
Shadow let us two walk.
Do you like this disjunctive talk?
Since we are now no longer under a friendly
Or even impartial arbiter of essence
We may think, in this drawing-in, of its strange veiling,
Not in inherited forms, of equestrian godlings
Or master going to bed or even
A benevolent source revolving, but rather
Of a nuclear engine got round a bend,
But that won't help us; and of that crescent
Not as the sky's sickle or nice Diana or even

Our tellurian sister younger and colder
But as a round rock out there,
And won't either. (See, the twig-ends
Are vapoured suddenly and all our timber
Mere clouds on sticks! All the wet green
Sky too has run out through that little fissure,
Showing the black bowl bare. It is chilly
Here in October, in this county
And corner of this county, cold as age,
As endless
And twice as friendless. . . .)

Have you noticed, by the way, it is growing chilly?
That could be predicted. Are you done predicting?
And we old. Let us speak of details.

That, when you come down to it, is all.
A question of region: they have unequal tongues,
Unequal weather,
One one and one another.
Here we speak elms and whitebeams and this chill,
And our rakes have teeth of iron, you may know us by this,
We are the animals of it. In Africa
Alternatively *tout ça change*. Excellent,
So long as it isn't a problem: we are done with problems.
The question is not to question but to inhabit
Wherever, whatever, we are, and all regions
Are good but
Religion is an ill region.

Do you like this disjunctive talk? No harm in it.
Yes, I am uncertain. If we are uncertain,
If we are poets we may make poems
Of the certainty of our uncertainty.

The wise go to their burrows and the warm.

Shall we turn in? The night, as I have said.
There are matters of soil and of what best there grows
In every sense, we are best concerned
With particular floras (step charily, in this dim
Air the way back is treacherous), it well may be
Thus we best praise what would be (were He) Him.

R. N. Currey

REMEMBERING SNOW

Today I think of a boy in the Transvaal
Spending his Christmas Day at the *krantzes*
Where the khaki drought of veld, cleft open,
Held festivals of water in a fern-green canyon.

We dived fork-naked into crystal pools,
Explored behind the maidenhair waterfalls,
Eating our Christmas pudding beneath the grace
Of feminine willows on the vivid grass.

My mother lured the pony with lumps of sugar;
We coaxed him into his creaking cat's-cradle of leather,
My father, all that tawny homeward run,
Remembering snow as I remember the sun.

Clifford Dyment

THE DESERT

Beside a dune high as a tree
　　But spreading no tree's shade
A man and boy sat silently
　　Working at their trade.

A heap of bones lay on the sand
　　Like barkless staves of wood;
And near it lay a second heap
　　Polished with thickening blood.

One bone, two bones, three bones were
　　Chosen by the man
Who made of them a heart's shape, wide
　　As his two hands would span.

The man and boy sat hour by hour
　　Calmly, coolly, dumb,
Feeling the scarlet heat as though
　　Their blackened skins were numb.

A third heap soon rose at their side
　　Like boughs laid for a pyre:
The boy's hand went to it and took
　　From many lyres one lyre.

It was a lyre in shape, but where
　　The stream of music springs
The lyre was nought, a mouth crying
　　Wordlessly for strings.

The boy reached to the heap that shone
    Untouched on the sand
And from its bloody muteness drew
    A bloody speaking hand.

He fixed the voice in place, then more,
    And soon the lyre was strung—
A frame made of three human bones,
    Each string a human tongue.

The old man took the brilliant lyre
    And struck its cords of red;
The boy rapt by his side stood up
    As a snake rears up its head

And with no smile and with no sigh
    Moved to the lyre's sounds
In a world all dust save for a man,
    A dancer, and three mounds.

Anthony Edkins

ADJUST YOUR DRESS
BEFORE LEAVING

The man, who is sidling towards me, has a worried look on his
face; he ignores my encouraging smile and whispers furtively:
'Excuse my mentioning it, but your trouser buttons are open.'
I close them.

The woman, meeting my greeting with perfunctory greeting,
observes, matter-of-factly:
'You have some egg in the corner of your mouth.'
I dislodge it with the tip of my tongue.

The lady, with unstill fluttering hands, talking the while, deftly
removes a hair from my lapel, saying:
'A hair!'
I bow.

The gentleman, aggressive, hearty, exclaims:
'I say, old boy, you've got some dust or something on your
    back.'
He pounds my shoulders heavily and shouts:
'That's better now!'
I arrange my coat.

Giggling nervously, the young lad opposite points out that one
of my socks is inside out.
I acknowledge this and right it.

Some time later an inspector says reprovingly:
'Your shoelace is undone.'
I do it up.

Sometimes during the day when I am driving oncoming motorists
sound their horns to signify the lights of my vehicle are on.
I switch them off and honk politely.
And sometimes at night they flash their lights to show me that my lights are off.
I switch them on, then dip them gratefully.

When I was a baby they altered my sleeping posture to avoid wind.

When I am dying the last words I expect to hear are:
'His breathing is irregular.'

Julian Ennis

HEDGEHOG

A hedgehog comes each twilight to my lawn
To eat the supper I put out,
Things it was, presumably, not born
To eat, things to give any hedgehog food for doubt.

The point is that we do not forget,
I to feed and he to come. We perform some rite,
Hold some communion, acknowledging our debt
To whatever brings us thus together in the night.

I pray for him, and for the owl that calls
From the big tree beyond my lawn, even though he
And the mere thought of all he is, appals,
Nauseates my soft humanity.

So I serve the shadows, try to grace
With offerings the challenge made
By hedgehogs, owls, all the race
Of remote beasts that in darkness raid

Me and my garden. I cultivate
Old terrors on this small scale,
The better, perhaps, to face the great
Ones later on, thorn and nail.

D. J. Enright

PITCHFORK DEPARTMENT

It was patent in this ancient city, paradise of
Statuary, that pigeons lacked respect for greatness.
Lucky statesmen, innocent generals and forgiven thinkers,

Their iron breasts befouled, their noble brows
Turned grey, their swords and croziers rusted,
Manuscripts illuminated, padded shanks gone leprous.

Yet the children loved the pigeons, it pleased the
Taxpayers to be used as perches. They walked our streets,
Sometimes were run over, did not despise our bread.

So the city fathers, as humane as is becoming
In this age of letters and elections, set out
Drugged fodder: 'Let the sleeping birds be stacked

With care in corporation vehicles, and conveyed to
Some remote and rural district. Let them there be laid
In appropriate positions in their proper places.'

They slept the weekend through, lost in a dream
Of the Hall of the 33,333 Buddhas, or the day
When every civil servant will be issued with a public statue.

On Tuesday afternoon, from under their umbrellas,
The city fathers watched the homing pigeons, assiduous, un-
    resenting,
Bowels gently stimulated, natural functions unaffected.

Roy Fuller

STARLING

Abandoning looks to art like a diva, the young
Starling opens its bill at an obscene
Angle, and squawks.

Not art but wrath, no doubt, at seeing the wrong
World: felines sprawled across his green-
Crusted pie of worms.

Was it this bather-sleek and quartz-flecked rowdy
Who later lay upon his back and showed
That beneath his arms

The upholstery in fact was dun and dowdy:
Disdained except by one extended bored
Tea-sipper's claw?

Kenneth Gee

LOCAL STORM

It may be near evening the sky turns sour
and thunder growls among the lilac trees;
someone stacking up the garden chairs
will notice how the early summer breeze

turns violent in a dirty smudge of cloud
sprung from an unexpected quarter; rain
unloads its little bombs of anger on
the lawn: the noonday sun has burned in vain.

The town is shuttered in its local darkness;
someone who is suffering from heartache
looks on the bending trees as signs of grieving;
if only overloaded boughs would break.

Even indoors they shelter from the sky
that spills its evil weight across the sill;
the animals are nervous; the wind through cracks
bears rumours that the sea has made a kill:

speaking with anxiety and wonder,
someone hopes the shower will do good;
though silently, people and flowers submit
to what was never really understood.

Robert Gittings

THE FOX

In the evening we reached the island of San Pedro, where we found the *Beagle* at anchor. In doubling the point, two of the officers landed to take a round of angles with the theodolite. A fox (*Canis fulvipes*) of a kind said to be peculiar to the island, and very rare in it, and which is a new species, was sitting on the rocks. He was so intently absorbed in watching the work of the officers, that I was able, by quietly walking up behind, to knock him on the head with my geological hammer.

CHARLES DARWIN, The Voyage of the Beagle

On the stone island, rough with rocks,
Tawny among the grey, a fox
Sat. Round his haunches the brush curled
Demurely as a pennant furled,
Signal of peace and self-won ease.
The spearflight of a wedge of geese
Hardly disturbed his sleekness, still
As a small cloud on a smooth hill,
Resting half-anchored. Then a shout
From the dull water echoes out.
He cocks an ear; his other sense
Through nose and eye gains evidence
Of movement on the shore. Some men,
Their boat dragged high, sea-booted, kin
To nothing on this desolate coast,
Stand earnestly about a post
Three-legged to their two. They probe,
And stoop, and peer along a tube
With purposeless intensity.
The fox cranes out his neck to see
What hunting or what play is this,
When from his back, descending hiss,
The hammer falls. A twitch, a leap,
The golden flanks are dead asleep

For ever, the inquisitive eye
Starting and glazed to eternity,
And Mr. Darwin, with a cough,
Scoops up the body and makes off,
Dangling another link to show
The fine mesh of his theory. So
Dies the live fox. The living man
Somehow will prove this nature's plan,
Selected by his larger skull
To crack the other. Pitiful
And far away the whole affair,
Yet breeding all dilemma there.
The animals of science have
Invaded life. The wise and brave
Are nothing or corrupted. Now
The mushroom cloud begins to grow.

Michael Hamburger

LIFE AND ART
(*For Denis Lowson*)

'A cell,' I reply when visitors remark
On the small high windows of the room I work in,
A room without a view. 'Exactly what I need,
Daylight enough—no more—to push a pen by,
And no distractions. Even the two great elms
With their congregations, race riots and social conflicts,
Endless commotion of squirrels, jackdaws and owls
Not to be seen, and only seldom heard.'

You dropped in one morning and sketched the garden,
All blue and black with the bulk and shade of those elms.
At once I longed to possess it. (The garden, the sketch?)
And above my desk I pinned up the silence extracted
From the endless commotion of squirrels, jackdaws and owls.
My garden hangs on the wall—and no distractions.

Christopher Hampton

SHRINE

What was I doing in this doll's house room?

I turned on my side to glance at the flowers
Faded in paper, pausing at the light-browned
Photograph portrait of a girl of six
Caught smiling over the mantelshelf.

The child stared at me, trapped in the frame,
Remote and hovering, frail as a humming-bird.
Small face, tight-curled hair with a ribbon,
Glimpse of flounced cotton party-frock——
Yellowed, ebbing in the chintzy light,
Shedding from the eyes faint quavers of laughter
That shivered in a glass and flickered the candle.

The room stilled echoes, privy to a childhood;
Left me oppressed and restive as in churches,
Watched by silence, by the not-quite-dead.

This little girl receding in a fat gold frame
(A child madonna charmed by a penny candle)
Edged across the room her vestige of a smile,
Like one who waits for worship and prayer.

I flinched away from her to watch the curtain
Flapping at the small deep window, lying still,
Evading the wilted inflections of her smile.
And I thought of the rain outside on the hills,
The water shivering in ditches, and the night
Subduing half the world, the nulled and shrineless,
From a quilt-covered bed in a flower-papered room,
With a small girl iconed smiling on a shelf.

John Hewitt

TURF CARRIER ON ARANMORE

The small boy drove the shaggy ass
out of the yard along the track,
rutted between two drystone walls,
his errand guessed from half-built stack.
Barefoot he tripped behind its tail,
too shy to lag and stride with us:
an older lad would match our pace
and snatch some topic to discuss.
He swung his switch, a salley rod,
his bleached head glinting in the sun,
but only flicked his ragged thighs
and pattered nonchalantly on.

We spoke no word. The boy, the ass,
the rutted path across the bare
unprofitable mountainside,
were native to this Druid air.
But, as we followed, rag and patch,
the string which braced each splintered creel,
the bald, rubbed flank, the hooves unshod,
growing awry and down-at-heel,
so woke our pity, I pronounced
a bitter sentence to condemn
the land that bred such boys and beasts
to starve the beauty out of them.

The small boy heard—not quite my words
but rather say—my angry tone;
a bright blush warmed his sunburnt neck;
he struck a sharp and jolting bone,
and turned the ass with prod and cry
through the first gap that caught his glance,

although the ruts roamed on ahead
to meet the bog's black-trenched expanse,
misjudging my intent and sure
that we were proud and critical.
Your father's beast is very dear,
if you are poor, if you are small.

John Holloway

CAFÉ DE LA MUSIQUE

It seems a cold blue star, the lamp in the square.
Hundreds of asteroid moths aimlessly circuit there.
Tired, I glance at her rings, the things in her lap,
As she chatters and fidgets and hunts all the time for a scrap
(Marionette) of paper to show me. As
I think, there is the lamp, with its halo of moths, and
Here I am, watching what dithers like splinters of glass,
And the midget conductor is dithering away at his band.

Yes, yes, I will look. But what do I see? The moth
Surface of faint down on her arm; the cloth
(Patiently pressed) of her dress; I notice the blue
On her ankle where it has rubbed on the side of her shoe
With the cobbler's obscure economical iron in the heel.
A moth lands on the table between us. No blaze
Of gold, but its real, leafy green. And the real
Woman unfolds before my discredited gaze.

'Look alive!' I say to myself; I watch her breath
As it ebbs and flows, and suddenly I see: death
Has only this for alternative—tentative tide
Like a dilating plant that opens wide
At last as a kind of light from its calyx of green
(Hark at that man, languishing his 'cello to sing!)
Not great blue star, fumbling moth. We have been
Dead photographic eye, and living thing.

AGE OF INNOCENCE

But did not paradise itself contain,
Sad embryo, hidden beneath its heart,
The whole of wrinkled history in a why?
For all the garden wondered; the first rain
Brought shimmering miracle; the waking earth
Lay a huge lovely question to the sky.

In that green kindergarten of the years
'Thou shalt not' seemed a crabbed unlikely tale.
She saw no dark forbiddings on the trees,
And if a suave snake whispered in her ears
She marvelled at the bright and pleated scales
And found his discourse natural as the breeze.

All was brand-new, and she was curious
For freckled mushrooms, waterfalls and fur,
And every light sweet flower-face, coloured stone;
Dazed by the tangled beauties could not choose;
Adoring every vein and every hair
She thought God's love as general as her own.

So Eve. And Adam's eyes already turned
To foresight. He would puzzle from the clouds
News of a falling chill or the wind's change,
Would ask the raving comets why they burned,
Call echoes from the silence of the woods,
Dig up new herbs, and joy to find them strange.

Sure, she was all too near the wanton earth,
Too like the breeze that visits everywhere;
And he too thirsty for the shifting sky.

Perhaps it had to be. It was their worth—
They drank it from the uncorrupted air—
To love, to wonder, and to disobey.

She never understood why she would cry
For hurts she had not felt—beyond all sense
These mother's griefs, and blood upon the ground.
He never told her of the night he lay
Beside her warm and breathing innocence,
And dreamed a face, tortured and mocked and crowned.

Ted Hughes

THISTLES

Against the rubber tongues of cows and the hoeing hands of men
Thistles spike the summer air
And crackle open under a blue-black pressure.

Every one a revengeful burst
Of resurrection, a grasped fistful
Of splintered weapons and Icelandic frost thrust up

From the underground stain of a decayed Viking.
They are like pale hair and the gutturals of dialects.
Every one manages a plume of blood.

Then they grow grey like men.
Mown down, it is a feud. Their sons appear
Stiff with weapons, fighting back over the same ground.

Ted Hughes

UNKNOWN SOLDIER

A gleam in a whisky head became a command.
Out of the opaque bubbling of England
The officer's face was a crystal. This refracted
The gleam and turned it to mathematics.

A sergeant thickened, stiffened to a body
Around the officer's aired word.
The ordinary privates stood in a herd.
They only had to hear and get ready.

This one, drugged with a hangover from
The draughts of courage they drank at home,
Dozed a little in a hopeful suppose.
Anything to avoid a fuss.

To luck he had already surrendered.
If life was going to play foul,
It could have the game, see if he cared.
Going with his mates was a goal meanwhile.

Until the brain that stands to right
Could find a rightful argument,
The monkey body didn't mind—
Finding plenty to imitate.

His life hung on a silk thread
Around his neck, with his name inscribed—
A good-luck charm to joke about,
A superstition, inherited.

Obscure was the command from the start
That took a bullet's spiritual arc
From the officer's throat through darkness
To jolt a mound of dirt.

G. W. Ireland

CLAUSTROPHOBIA

My father in his prime: a wall of muscle,
A wall of silence.

Winning always, but not unmindful
Of those the pit had killed before his eyes
And in his absence behind walls of wrack,
His smile was guarded; it was not begrudged,
As little compromising as his frown.

When the smile first trembled, the abdominal wall
Was granite and convincing. To the eyes
I could not raise my eyes.

But after forty years of sleep
Peremptorily claimed, he could not sleep.

I heard him in the night.

Yet he was always perfectly discreet
And spoke as if he went on mining coal
As overweening still as Alexander.
Until he broke.

His nights were haunted by his haunted days,
He wept and shivered, clinging to the wife
For forty proud years he had towered beside
And begged her only give these fears a name.

The doctor knew a most impressive name
Which my father could not pronounce.
A well-meant humour lies upon his tongue

(He knew my father well): You're not a gardener!
But why not take up . . . bowls? A grand game, man . . .
You know as well as I . . . but what's the use
Telling you, forty years gone,
A handful still to go, to keep yourself
Out of dark, close places.

Ada Jackson

AUNT ABIGAIL

Aunt Abigail was practical
and liked things done on time;
unhurried and in order, true
to pattern as a rhyme.

So when she saw that Uncle John
would not get up again,
her coat went to the dyer's and
she sold a laying hen

to buy a hank of knitting silk;
and set without delay
to make a mourning scarf to wear
upon his burial day.

He had a splendid funeral;
no relative but said
the whole thing was a credit to
the living and the dead.

A day for long remembering—
but I shall only see
Aunt Abby in a bedside chair,
a-knitting steadily;

Aunt Abby casting off her rows
with silk and time to spare—
and two old eyes that cleared, and saw
what she was doing there.

Coaches, wreaths and bearers' names—
I shall forget them all;
but not my uncle's stricken face,
turned silent to the wall.

Elizabeth Jennings

ONE FLESH

Lying apart now, each in a separate bed,
He with a book, keeping the light on late,
She like a girl dreaming of childhood,
All men elsewhere—it is as if they wait
Some new event: the book he holds unread,
Her eyes fixed on the shadows overhead.

Tossed up like flotsam from a former passion,
How cool they lie. They hardly ever touch,
Or if they do it is like a confession
Of having little feeling—or too much.
Chastity faces them, a destination
For which their whole lives were a preparation.

Strangely apart and strangely close together,
Silence between them like a thread to hold
And not wind in. And time itself's a feather
Touching them gently. Do they know they're old,
These two who are my father and my mother
Whose fire, from which I came, has now grown cold?

Elizabeth Jennings

THE DIAMOND CUTTER

Not what the light will do but how he shapes it
And what particular colours it will bear.

And something of the climber's concentration
Seeing the white peak, setting the right foot there.

Not how the sun was plausible at morning
Nor how it was distributed at noon,

And not how much the single stone could show
But rather how much brilliance it would shun;

Simply a paring down, a cleaving to
One object, as the star-gazer who sees

One single comet polished by its fall
Rather than countless, untouched galaxies.

Glyn Jones

MORNING

On the night beach, quiet beside the blue
Bivouac of sea-wood, and fresh loaves, and the
Fish baking, the broken Ghost, whose flesh burns
Blessing the dark bay and the still mast-light,
Shouts, 'Come'.

        A naked man on deck who heard
Also cockcrow, turning to the pebbles, sees
A dawn explode among the golden boats,
Pulls on his sea-plaid, leaps into the sea.

Wading the hoarfrost meadows of that fiord's
Daybreak, he, hungering fisherman, forgets
Cockcrow tears, dark noon, dead god, empty cave,
All those mountains of miraculous green
Light that swamped the landing-punt, and kneels,
Shivering, in a soaked blouse, eating by the
Blue blaze the sweet breakfast of forgiveness.

THE PAY IS GOOD

A class of thirty student engineers,
Sixteen years old, disliked by all the staff.
Hearing about them at the interview,
And told to rule them with a rod of iron,
I tried my best but found I could not laugh.

He might be wrong. But I, no raw recruit,
Had found a proverb in a classroom war:
The peaceful sheriff proves that he can shoot
Before he throws his gunbelt on the floor.

A month or so of brooding self-distrust,
And then the moment came. I reached the door
(So this is it. Fight, for the love of Kell.
Show them who's boss—there's no going back—
            you must)—
And flung it open on the core of hell.

Somehow it worked. And they will never know
By what dissimulation it was done;
Or how the fuse of terror blasted out
Courage enough to master thirty-one.

Francis King

A LIE FOR THE FUTURE

When you are fifty-five or sixty-five
  (Quite soon), when fewer people turn to stare,
And fear of death alone keeps you alive;
    With thickening waist-line and with thinning hair
      'At least,' you then will think, 'one does not falter,
      One does not fall away, one does not alter'.

A lie, of course, a lie; for I long since
  Shall have begun to rail against the waste
Of days and of devotion and to wince
  At all your faults of vanity and taste.
      'Most things,' I'll think then, 'come to those who wait,
      But come too stale and shop-soiled, come too late.'

But which of us will voice these truths or dare
  Admit to folly? Which have strength to break
Habits as all-encompassing as air?
    Rather, each silent for our lost love's sake,
      Won't we prefer, as friends and years grow fewer,
      Still one to act pursued and one pursuer?

Thomas Kinsella

THE LAUNDRESS

Her chair drawn to the door,
A basket at her feet,
She sat against the sun
And stitched a linen sheet.
Over harrowed Flanders
August moved the wheat.

Poplars sharing the wind
With Saxony and France
Dreamed at her gate,
Soared in a Summer trance.
A cluck in the cobbled yard:
A shadow changed its stance.

As a fish cleaves the pond
And sinks without a stain
The heels of ripeness fluttered
Under her apron. Then
Her heart grew strained and light
As the shell that shields the grain.

Bluntly through the doorway
She stared at shed and farm,
At yellow fields unstitching
About the hoarded germ,
At land that would spread white
When she had reached her term.

The sower plumps his acre,
Flanders turns to the heat,
The winds of Heaven winnow
And the wheels grind the wheat.
She searched in her basket
And fixed her ruffled sheet.

James Kirkup

THE POET'S BIOGRAPHIES

'Happiest Alone', 'The Countermask', etc. Rather a mess, the
Book-club titles. The chumps get most of the facts, of course—
The correct birthday, more or less,
Christening and marriages, divorces, on the dot:
And, dead right, the day of death.
Letters, journals (so cutting), yes.
But some things now can not
Be verified at source:
Things the beat-up bard himself forgot
Till past his final breath.

Though he so careless and unaccountable
Of reputation, they only choose
To make him a bit respectable.
Despair of reviewers, hating to belong
To groups or gangs or anything with neatness,
His 'champions' always get it slightly wrong,
Bringing him 'into perspective', lose
The elusive thing that made his song;
'Seeing the whole man,' miss his incompleteness.

How can he ever tell those 'dedicated' ones
He wasn't altogether
What they claim he was: of his bones
Are morals made, nothing of him
Who never knew, or cared
If he was doing right or wrong—a dim
Sense of decency his only tether
In a world where he was never in the swim,
That feigned a tenderness he never shared.

Dead, he keeps his secrets:
Those long months when he couldn't do a thing
But sleep, drink, giggle or throw chocolates
At the ceiling: those moments at dead of night
When the drug left him shivering alone
On the horrid brink of light—
Things he would never have dreamt of putting
Down in words, or telling. Well, now he's gone.
Only he would have got it really right.

FAITH HEALING

Slowly the women file to where he stands
Upright in rimless glasses, silver hair,
Dark suit, white collar. Stewards tirelessly
Persuade them onwards to his voice and hands,
Within whose warm spring rain of loving care
Each dwells some twenty seconds. *Now, dear child,*
What's wrong, the deep American voice demands,
And, scarcely pausing, goes into a prayer
Directing God about this eye, that knee.
Their heads are clasped abruptly; then, exiled

Like losing thoughts, they go in silence; some
Sheepishly stray, not back into their lives
Just yet; but some stay stiff, twitching and loud
With deep hoarse tears, as if a kind of dumb
And idiot child within them still survives
To re-awake at kindness, thinking a voice
At last calls them alone, that hands have come
To lift and lighten; and such joy arrives
Their thick tongues blort, their eyes squeeze grief, a crowd
Of huge unheard answers jam and rejoice—

What's wrong! Moustached in flowered frocks they shake:
By now, all's wrong. In everyone there sleeps
A sense of life lived according to love.
To some it means the difference they could make
By loving others, but across most it sweeps
As all they might have done had they been loved.
That nothing cures. An immense slackening ache,
As when, thawing, the rigid landscape weeps,
Spreads slowly through them—that, and the voice above
Saying *Dear child*, and all time has disproved.

Michael Levien

IN THE FALLING DEER'S MOUTH

In the falling deer's mouth
There runs a dark river,
Furred by blue moss.
Hammered into his bones
With the silver shot
That stumbled his stride
Are pines, leaves, and birds.

He was wild this tall prince
Whose antlers spired forests.
Curled, his sharp crown
Thonged his rivals to earth.
And he pierced the night
With stars on his hooves,
His eyes gathered bats

And the nightingales crept
His ears with ripe, summer
Chimes. So wild, free,
Sprang the shoots of his limbs
That the hunter held
His ravaging aim,
His eyes dipped in dreams.

In the falling deer's mouth
There spills a live mirror,
Flushed by green roots.
Frozen into his skull
With the crimson wound
That shivered his blood
Are pines, leaves, and birds.

Edward Lucie-Smith

ON LOOKING AT STUBBS'S
ANATOMY OF THE HORSE

In Lincolnshire, a village full of tongues
Not tired by a year's wagging, and a man
Shut in a room where a wrecked carcass hangs,
His calm knife peeling putrid flesh from bone;
He whistles softly, as an ostler would;
The dead horse moves, as if it understood.

That night a yokel holds the taproom still
With tales new-hatched; he's peeped, and seen a mare
Stand there alive with naked rib and skull—
The creature neighed, and stamped upon the floor;
The warlock asked her questions, and she spoke;
He wrote her answers down in a huge book . . .

Two centuries gone, I have the folio here,
And turn the pages, find them pitiless.
These charts of sinew, vein and bone require
A glance more expert, more detached than this—
Fingering the margins, I think of the old
Sway-backed and broken nags the pictures killed.

Yet, standing in that room, I watched the knife;
Light dances on it as it maps a joint
Or scribes a muscle; I am blank and stiff,
The blade cuts so directly to my want;
I gape for anecdote, absurd detail,
Like any yokel with his pint of ale.

George MacBeth

THE COMPASSES

Baroque-handled and sharp
With blunt lead in their lips
And their fluted legs together
My father's compasses
Lie buried in this flat box.

I take it out of its drawer,
Snap old elastic bands
And rub the frayed leatherette:
It smells faintly of smoke:
The broken hinges yawn.

As I level the case to look
A yellowed protractor claps
Against black-papered board,
Sliding loose in the lid
Behind a torn silk flap.

I look in the base at the dusty
Velvet cavities;
Dead-still, stiff in the joints
And side by side they lie
Like armoured knights on a tomb.

One by one I lift
Them out in the winter air
And wipe some dust away:
Screw back their gaping lips
And bend the rigid knees.

In an inch of hollowed bone
Two cylinders of lead
Slither against each other
With a faint scurrying sound.
I lay them carefully back

And close the case. In Crookes
My father's bones are scattered
In a measured space of ground:
Given his flair for drawing
These compasses should be there

Not locked away in a box
By an uninstructed son
But like an Egyptian king's
Ready shield and swords
Beside his crumbling hand.

Roy Macnab

THE HIPPOPOTAMUS

Out of the Zulu bush one day she came,
Without a by-your-leave, it was good-bye
To the hills of Mapumulo, the herd and St. Lucia Bay,
A bellow on the wind and dust in the air,
Through broken mealies, the shattered stalks of cane,
Into our world the hippopotamus came.

Two years the journey, two thousand miles
In bush and swamp, in cities, the pages of *Punch*
And *The Times*, stirred by ancestral memories, they said,
Searching for a long-lost ego; though once at night
In the dead-quiet street and the window's light,
She saw herself whole and took fright.

But never turned back to the past, the taste
Came soon for lights and fame, one day
At noon from the river's bed late rising,
She walked the square with councillor and mayor,
And ate three fields of Pondo's fare, who thought
Thus to placate a much-feared witch.

Ours the accolade came next, the royal game, we too
Made much of her who on dignity and maize grew fat,
At many a muddy spa taking the waters, the sophisticate
Was quite unprepared for the dénouement;
In the morning papers, with some surprise, we read
Of a sticky end, at Keiskama, two bullets in the head.

Questions in Parliament and mourning, the assassins
Brought to court, there was nothing mean, I remember,
About the passing of Huberta, the celebrity's head

Stood firm on the courtroom table, later for posterity
With its nether self rejoined, was put down for parade
Here in the museum at Kingwilliamstown.

Now twenty-five years later as we stand, my child,
You in another generation, would that I could
Draw you but back beyond the taxidermist's art,
To where once and for once the fabulous tale came true,
When the great beast walked each night through the nursery
    dream,
Only to leave, when daylight came, a garden of wrecked
    cabbages.

Louis MacNeice

THE WIPER

Through purblind night the wiper
Reaps a swathe of water
On the screen: we shudder on
    And hardly hold the road,
All we can see a segment
Of blackly shining asphalt
With the wiper moving across it
    Clearing, blurring, clearing.

But what to say of the road?
The monotony of its hardly
Visible camber, the mystery
    Of its far invisible margins,
Will these be always with us,
The night being broken only
By lights that pass or meet us
    From others in moving boxes?

Boxes of glass and water,
Upholstered, equipped with dials
Professing to tell the distance
    We have gone, the speed we are going,
But never a gauge or needle
To tell us where we are going
Or when day will come, supposing
    This road exists in daytime.

For now we cannot remember
Where we were when it was not
Night, when it was not raining,
    Before this car moved forward

And the wiper backward and forward
Lighting so little before us
Of a road that, crouching forward,
   We watch move always towards us,

Which through the tiny segment
Cleared and blurred by the wiper
Is sucked in under our wheels
   To be spewed behind us and lost
While we, dazzled by darkness,
Haul the black future towards us
Peeling the skin from our hands;
   And yet we hold the road.

Adrian Mitchell

THE DUST

Singing, as she always must,
Like the kitten-drowner with a howling sack,
Open-eyed through the shallow dust
Goes the dust-coloured girl with a child on her back.

A schoolgirl in a flowered dress,
Swayed by the swaying of a tree
And the sun's grin, in front of her family
One day became a prophetess.

Like a singer who forgets her song
She awkwardly leant from the graceful chair,
Balanced her fists in the drawing-room air
And said that everyone was wrong, that she was wrong.

Shocked by this infantile mistake
Her uncles and aunts were sad to find
This ugly girl with an ugly mind
In a house as rich as birthday cake.

When the bombs fell, she was sitting with her man
Straight and white in the family pew.
While in her the bud of a child grew,
The city crumbled, the deaths began.

Now, singing as she always must,
A refugee from a love burned black,
Open-eyed through the rising dust
Goes the dust-coloured girl with a child on her back.

DIALOGUE VII:
HAKUIN[1] AND CHIKAMATSU[2]

HAKUIN

When I first came to Suruga, it was worse.
A hopeless roof, the stars looked through it at night.
Debts, mortgages everywhere. The best bell cracked.
We're still a poor temple, but not ruinous.
Hard work is good for novices' backs; they got
More than they bargained for, those that I took in—
Begging to be bowled along to buddhahood!
I showed them Buddha: a bit of broken brick.
—It was an afternoon like this when I came,
But now the sun seems more brilliant, so brilliant
It almost strikes the bell into chimes; the lake
It almost breaks like glass as it lies flashing.
The heart could be lost in this heat and silence.
Perhaps the days of leaking roofs are the best?

CHIKAMATSU

Sitting here in the cool of the veranda,
With the temple cat and a tobacco-tray,
We might indeed lose sense of reality—
Unless this is reality, and a man
Who shakes the dust of cities off as you do
Should surely find it is? A danger for me,
But why should heat and silence trouble hermits?
I need Osaka, the tea-houses and throngs,

---

[1] Hakuin (1685–1768), Japanese Buddhist sage and teacher, 'the founder of modern Zen'.
[2] Chikamatsu (1653–1725), 'the Japanese Shakespeare', writer of popular plays for the puppet theatre.

The theatres, the turning pleasure-lanterns,
The cries and smells headier than temple-bells.
Here, I drowse to the last insignificance.
Are you afraid of your own meditations?
You have brought your heart here; how can you lose it?

HAKUIN

The heart is lost in attachment to the sun,
Or to any place, or to any person,
Or to any thing but illumination,
And that is not attachment. The heart is lost
By love. Love of this place would make the mind dark,
Clouded by a barren solicitousness.
'The cherry is late; these stones should be regrouped;
Shall we lacquer the dishes red this year?'
Enlightened monks I want, not geishas. A bowl,
A mat, a stick, a brain, a space to breathe in,
And all the paradoxes shall clap their hands
As if this silent play was Chikamatsu's.

CHIKAMATSU

Reality, then, is neither here nor there?

HAKUIN

But what are the paradoxes clapping at?

CHIKAMATSU

I might ask, what are the creatures clapping *with*?

HAKUIN

May I enrol you as a student of Zen?
Your questions are promising. But start from this.
What is the sound of the clapping of one hand?

The theatre's empty. What, have you gone home?

Good, good! But look now, no hands.

                                        A thunderclap,
Rather far off, do you hear it? And the flash—

Basho's poem: seventeen syllables: *O*
Sudden lightning, and down the darkness the scream
Of the night heron!—Yet you ask, what is Zen?

A poet's imagination is a help.
Make poets monks, and Zen will soar up, right off.
Enlightenment will come in constellations.
The world will be miles down, struggling, in a net.
What is meditation, to a metaphor!
But then where are you? Where's your reality?
When mystics are eloquent, the faith teeters.
You should be glad I am only a playwright.
Keep the ineffable on the prayer-mat,
With rice and chopsticks, but neither brush nor ink;
When the lightning strikes, let it not speak, just think.
The night heron that screams the gloom to tatters
May choke on the majestic lie it utters.
—Reality, reality! people cry.
All right. The dramatist tries realism.
Some years ago Osaka thrilled to the news
Of a suicide-pact—a young apprentice
And a poor tea-house girl he couldn't marry:

He cut her throat in the Sonezaki Woods,
Then cut his own; they were found bound to one tree.
Within a fortnight *Sonezaki Shinju*,
My play of this event, was staged; applauded;
By all Osaka; O, a play of such truth—
But was it truth? Did they blow out the lantern
As I said they did? Did the maid striking flints
Cover their escape by a creaking door-hinge?
And were they a model for all true lovers
As the last line stated? My fleshless actors
Were puppets of pine, their gesticulations
Were generalizations, their passions poured
From a hidden throat and a thin samisen.
Ah, what was left of the Sonezaki Woods?
Did I show what was suffered there? Did I die?
—If those who bled on the tree were not silent,
If those who speak could bleed on the truthful tree!

HAKUIN

Yet the truth comes to you as it comes to me.
The thud of snow in the forest, like a blow,
A whittrick at a harvest in Hokkaido,
Osaka watching a doll weep at a show.
For the doll does weep; men know.

CHIKAMATSU

And that is Zen?

HAKUIN

But what is Zen? You think it's either the case
'A doll can't cry' or 'I saw the doll crying'?
Are you going to renounce your own power?
Neither you nor I can be wholly truthful,
Though the truth comes to me as it comes to you.
Nor can your audience; nor my disciples.
Yet the truth comes.

                              Then why do we let it go?
Why in a world of doubts do we let it go?
Why do we let this heaven dissolve and go?

HAKUIN

When I was twenty-four I was Zenward-bound.
I fasted haggard as a wolf, refused sleep,
Sat unshaven shivering upon a board,
Kicked the paradoxes round my memory,
Stripped the jests and ferocities to meekness.
Static I became, brain-bound, ghostly, in chains;
Felt I was freezing at the silent centre
Of an ice-field stretching for millions of miles;
Slumped there like stalagmite, featureless and numb,
A fragment, naked, stupid, vulnerable,
Ghostly and vulnerable as a crystal.
Suddenly I heard the monastery bell.
The ice exploded with great cracks, my body
Burst from its crystal shell which fell like a shawl.
It was as if a tower of jade was smashed
To drops of living water. I moved, I rose.
I shouted out 'Wonderful, O wonderful!'
There was no perfect knowledge to starve after.
I had broken through to the life I left from.
Buddha dissolved in the water of the snow.
—And so I let this heaven dissolve and go.

CHIKAMATSU

And so you find it everywhere, like the air?

HAKUIN

Seize it: it's gone. It will not be seized again.

CHIKAMATSU

A shout in the street? A tea-house in the rain?

HAKUIN

Will you have some tea?

CHIKAMATSU

Yes. Thanks!

HAKUIN

This too is Zen.

Betty Parvin

TIME AND TIDE

Harebells within the chalk stones lie
Whose bonny bone my bloom will don;
Their filmy root my hair will tie,
My ebbing will enrich their dye
That breaks where I am gone

For on my palm a harebell—see
How flesh to flesh the veining runs!
This calyx is the wave of me
That from the creviced rock broke free,
These stamens are my sons.

William Plomer

LIME-FLOWER TEA

The esplanade empty, closed at this time
   The gates of the park;
The sea waveless, only a murmur
   In the formless dark
Of a night in winter; frost fusing
   Glass beads of drifted snow,
Trashy remnants of a white glare
   One dazzling day ago.

Frost hardens, glazes, grips; on glass
   Will damascene
Traceries tonight of ferns.
   A plain screen
Of fog has curtained off the sea.
   Street lamps illuminate
A livid emptiness, and one man,
   Only one, walking late.

He stops walking, stands then, vaguely gazing
   Is amazed to hear
Gentle flutings of seabirds,
   Unseen but near—
Communings of pure confidence,
   Intimations of their ease
And of a separate togetherness
   No arctic night could freeze.

Each flute-note has made him think
   Of his own life—
Quiet years with a neurotic
   Childless wife:

On a winter night when needling frost
   In total silence etches ferns,
He to her like a seabird speaks,
   She, wingless, to him turns.

His walk alone at night she understands
   And the unsaid;
In the warm room she'll pour out,
   Before bed,
Delicately, lime-flower tea;
   Together they will sip and dream,
Sad and content, both drugged
   By the lost summer in the scented steam.

Jonathan Price

A CONSIDERED REPLY TO A CHILD

'I love you,' you said between two mouthfuls of pudding.
But not funny; I didn't want to laugh at all.
Rolling three years' experience in a ball,
You nudged it friendlily across the table.

A stranger, almost, I was flattered—no kidding.
It's not every day I hear a thing like that;
And when I do my answer's never pat.
I'm about nine times your age, ten times less able

To say—what you said; incapable of unloading
Plonk at someone's feet, like a box of bricks,
A declaration. When I try, it sticks
Like fish-bones in my throat; my eyes tingle.

What's called 'passion', you'll learn, may become 'overriding'.
But not in me it doesn't: I'm that smart,
I can give everything and keep my heart.
Kisses are kisses. No need for souls to mingle.

Bed's bed, what's more, and you'd say it's meant for sleeping;
And, believe me, you'd be absolutely right.
With luck you'll never lie awake all night,
Someone beside you (rather like 'crying') weeping.

DISGUISE

Coat over arm I step off the moss-silenced stairs
On to thick turf that drains noise
And makes the heaviest walk like shadows; I
Have fat that hangs over me like heavy clothes
In wet sobbing creases, and I dash the sweat away like flies.
What do the people around see besides?
A young head, small and bony, smooth and rosy,
Nipple-pated to the shirt-bright paunch,
As I'm well aware, and people are upset by characters;
I have a body thirty years my senior.

House with grounds. . . .
Very well then, I will join the scene,
Join in by subterfuge; the lake's attractive
With the lilies massed like flock beds near
The strutted wooden bridge, an ornament,
That skips to the birdhouse on the marooned island.
I thumb the ground past faster. I will join the scene,
But not before I've bent with kilting paunch
To pry this midge out of the water-drop,
And held it out on pencil-point, clung like a wet feather,
Into the breeze to dry,
Struggling to its lashes, frail diagram.

The lazy bench-beams wheeze to me as I shake off my tie,
Unleash my neck, breath hissing hard, buried heart pounding,
Lean back and watch the shadows sliding through the lake,
And think of it iced, cool sheets and plates,
And see the flame has gripped the chestnuts,
Hear the wind hiss through them, and close my eyes,
Spread a clean handkerchief slowly over my face. . . .

And look the part, an old gentleman relaxing
On his accustomed bench in unswept leaves,
Relaxing to the leaf-hiss, braces swooping
Round calm stoutness in the dottle of the year,
Only the margin of the white cloth fluttering—
A gentle snoozing laid beneath a cloth—
Only quick coolnesses from people passing close.

THE TRAVELLERS

Approve the traveller who never went;
Slippers and timetables supply his want.

Admire the traveller who went, and stayed,
Renewing life in some rare latitude.

Honour the traveller who went, and died,
Raised above gain or failure by the deed.

But the returning traveller with a store
Of memoirs and an ancient-mariner stare

Shall be discredited from bar to bar
And in the end account himself a bore.

Vernon Scannell

PERSONAL INTERVIEW

'Listeners might be interested to hear
This programme where the greatest man of letters,
And possibly the greatest man in any
Sphere of intellectual endeavour,
Speaks frankly from the wisdom gathered over
Seventy years or so. This mellow store,
I'm sure will edify and entertain
Without imposing on us too much strain.
We're speaking from the great man's lovely home
And seated in a splendid book-lined room. . . .'

Eight million listeners act their patient role.
They listen. The sharp young voice begins to probe,
Fastidious but assured; the old one answers,
Dusty, frail. One almost smells the mould
Of yellow pages, but no illumination
Brightens bed-sitter, drawing-room or kitchen.
The sentiments are trite, the phrasing dull.
The stout words with their double chins wheeze out:
The Absolute, the True, the Beautiful.
Then as time wastes, the mouth begins to utter
Dry syllables that flutter like hurt moths.

Determined not to fail, the interviewer
Affects a brisker tone, a little too
Like a policeman's for this interview:
'Now you, sir, as a most exceptional man
Who's brooded long and deep on what goes on
Upon this earth and in the human heart,
Perhaps you'd tell us now what you believe
About the life to come beyond the grave.'

A silence seems to chill the air and threaten
The listener in his armchair or warm kitchen,
And then the great man speaks, quite clearly now,
'Get out of here! Get out, you prying fool!
Let in the death men in their soft black boots
Who come with measuring instruments to prove
I'm no exception to their iron rule.'

Vernon Scannell

THE TELEPHONE NUMBER

Searching for a lost address I find,
Among dead papers in a dusty drawer,
A diary which has lain there quite ten years,
And soon forget what I am looking for,
Intrigued by cryptic entries in a hand
Resembling mine but noticeably more
Vigorous than my present quavering scrawl.
Appointments—kept or not, I don't remember—
With people now grown narrow, fat or bald;
A list of books that somehow I have never
Found the time to read, nor ever shall,
Remind me that my world is growing cold.
And then I find a scribbled code and number,
The urgent words: 'Must not forget to call.'
But now, of course, I have no recollection
Of telephoning anyone at all.

The questions whisper: Did I dial that number
And, if I did, what kind of voice replied?
Questions that will never find an answer
Unless—the thought is serpentine—I tried
To telephone again, as years ago
I did, or meant to. What would I find
If now I lifted this mechanic slave
Black to my ear and spun the dial—so. . . . ?
Inhuman, impolite, the double burp
Erupts, insulting hope. The long dark sleeve
Of silence stretches out. No stranger's voice
Slips in, suspicious, cold; no manic speech

Telling what I do not wish to know,
Nor throaty message creamed with sensual greed—
Nothing of these. And when again I try,
Doodling foolish in a draughty need,
Relief is tearful when there's no reply.

E. J. Scovell

TIMES OF LIFE

No longer the unbridled crying, near or far,
Of little children calls me, their archaic voices.
I know they are not mine—whose learned weeping presses
Like ours against a heavy door;

Who are not always near, in the lap, in the house's hollow,
In the cradle mind; but free among the circling flocks
Now write on field and street invisible their tracks,
Paths on the air of lark or swallow.

My thought dwells on those trails, picks out and silvers them.
But the cries of infants knock and yet must house elsewhere—
From road or neighbouring garden filling a world of air
Like wail of lambs from a mountain stream.

WAS HE MARRIED?

Was he married? Did he try
To support as he grew less fond of them
Wife and family?

No,
He never suffered such a blow.

Did he feel pointless, feeble and distrait,
Unwanted by everyone and in the way?

From his cradle he was purposeful,
His bent strong and his mind full.

Did he love people very much
Yet find them die one day?

He did not love in the human way.

Did he ask how long it would go on,
Wonder if Death could be counted on for an end?

He did not feel like this,
He had a future of bliss.

Did he never feel strong
Pain for being wrong?

He was not wrong, he was right,
He suffered from others', not his own, spite.

But there *is* no suffering like having made a mistake
Because of being of an inferior make.

He was not inferior,
He was superior.

He knew then that power corrupts but some must govern?

His thoughts were different.

Did he lack friends? Worse,
Think it was for his fault, not theirs?

He did not lack friends,
He had disciples he moulded to his ends.

Did he feel over-handicapped sometimes, yet must draw even?

How could he feel like this? He was the King of Heaven.

. . . find a sudden brightness one day in everything
Because a mood had been conquered, or a sin?

I tell you, he did not sin.

Do only human beings suffer from the irritation
I have mentioned? learn too that being comical
Does not ameliorate the desperation?

Yes, only human beings feel this,
It is because they are so mixed.

All human beings should have a medal,
A god cannot carry it, he is not able.

A god is Man's doll, you ass,
He makes him up like this on purpose.

He might have made him up worse.

He often has, in the past.

To choose a god of love, as he did and does,
Is a little move then?

Yes, it is.

A larger one will be when men
Love love and hate hate but do not deify them?

It will be a larger one.

Margaret Stanley-Wrench

THE TOAD

On the black ridge of the road
Dank yellow oozed a toad.
The rain-wet, steaming wood
Stretched, his ultimate good,
But simple, primaeval, he
Bulked there, content to be.

And we, whose thoughts outrace
Our wheels and our own pace
Stopped, seeing that clot of yellow
Whose life to ours was fellow.
A knop of being, whose cold
Skin throbbed with the heart it held.

The slow peace of the wood,
The drip of the rain like blood,
All this for a moment became
Our life, as too, for him,
Nothing beyond the breath,
Life springing from the fungus death.

Taking him in our hand
We lifted him beyond
The black ridge of the road.
And then we knew, the toad
Was compassion, the weight we hold,
Warm heart in a rind of cold.

MY OLD CAT

My old cat is dead,
Who would butt me with his head.
He had the sleekest fur.
He had the blackest purr.
Always gentle with us
Was this black puss,
But when I found him today
Stiff and cold where he lay
His look was a lion's,
Full of rage, defiance:
Oh, he would not pretend
That what came was a friend
But met it in pure hate.
Well died, my old cat.

Donald Thomas

APOTHEOSIS

Impressed on metal and revealed in stone,
The emperor endures. Stamped profile poised
Or silent gesture marks the man whose face
Endorsed all current gold; for whom alone
The polished legions wheeled and gods deployed.
His was the shrewdest choice of time and place.

Others fought dry campaigns; he was on hand
To play slick cards for power: ace took the trick
And law was his. He whispered names and, quick
As knife, generals were carrion in the sand.

Packed to the echo in that silent city,
Arenas marked the nerve-end of his power;
Their dark-skinned grapplers and their family clowns
Banished to temples. At his oratory
The veterans rocked the arches with their roar
And offered him again the dead men's crowns.

Two galaxies of stars set to collide:
Ape born to courtesan: news indicates
An evil past control. Crossed by such fates,
Gods die like gangsters on the losing side.

The moment of the trap in action came:
A circle of his friends ringed him for death
And knives were out. Time for the fade-out scene,
A last salute, a cloak to muffle shame,
As blades encroached to punctuate his breath.
Then squads with wisecracks swilled the paving clean.

R. S. Thomas

NINETIETH BIRTHDAY. HILL FARM

You go up the long track,
That will take a car but is best climbed
On slow foot, noting the lichen
That writes history on the page
Of the grey rock. Trees are about you
At first, but yield to the green bracken,
The nightjar's house: you can hear it spin
On warm evenings; it is still now
In the noonday heat, only the lesser
Voices sound, blue-fly and gnat
And the stream's whisper. As the road climbs,
You will pause for breath and the far sea's
Signal will flash, till you turn again
To the steep track, buttressed with cloud.

And there at the top that old woman,
Born almost a century back
In that stone farm, awaits your coming,
Waits for the news of the lost village
She thinks she knows, a place that exists
In her memory only.
                                    You bring her greeting
And praise for having lasted so long
With time's ache sharp in her bones.
But no bridge joins her own
World with yours; all you can do
Is lean kindly across the abyss
To hear words that were once wise.

Anthony Thwaite

AT BIRTH

Come from a distant country,
Bundle of flesh, of blood,
Demanding painful entry,
Expecting little good:
There is no going back
Among those thickets where
Both night and day are black
And blood's the same as air.

Strangely you come to meet us,
Stained, mottled, as if dead:
You bridge the dark hiatus
Through which your body slid
Across a span of muscle,
A breadth my hand can span.
The gorged and brimming vessel
Flows over, and is man.

Dear daughter, as I watched you
Come crumpled from the womb,
And sweating hands had fetched you
Into this world, the room
Opened before your coming
Like water struck from rocks
And echoed with your crying
Your living paradox.

Sydney Tremayne

WIND SHAKES THE HOUSE

Again it moves, that millrace sweep of air;
Gales wrench the trees, a deep, continuous roar
Floods through the dark, and ebbs, and flings again
Wind of a solid force and thudding rain.
Half in, half out, my sheltered senses fly.
Drowning in air I filled my lungs to cry
My first breath back on such a night of noise,
Then through a month of storms that tore up trees
I slept, woke, slept, knowing neither world nor me,
Nursed in the void preceding memory's eye.
Tonight is like recovering by ear
Rhythm of breathing, as the wind draws near
In a long gust that rakes from the world's end
And shakes the house, making the windows bend
To which involuntarily I look to see
Some speck, some print that is not washed away
But catch instead my own face, two wars old.
Put out the light: the blinded spirit's pulled
Into the darkness where it cannot live.
Black chaos bound together like a wave
Slides without breaking over freezing space.
Enter the rage within the body's house,
Warm, squalling brat. The storm beats at the door
(Waves in a shell), the house yours to explore:
Its twisting corridors, its whispering stairs,
Junk, dust and damp, and unidentified smears.

Gael Turnbull

A HILL

Black upon orange, a profile of giant rubble, for a moment it barricades the sun. Orange out of black, a foliage of wrinkled copper, for a moment dawn germinates in a furrow of the hill.

The phrases are apt. The scene is not unusual. The joy is in the attention.

The description is not a circumscribed likeness; that is, of any delimited hill. It is not that, nor is it exactly at random.

The description portrays a hill which is discovered in the action; an unknown hill which becomes known, which is a likeness, and which becomes likely.

It is Bredon Hill. It is a name. But it is not that.

It is a whale, dark indigo, partly submerged, the dorsum crusted with shell-fish. And it is not.

It is Mount Badon, with Arthur and the company of the Table, and the last outpost of Empire, and the onrush of the barbarians up the Severn and Avon, with Tewkesbury burning. And it is not.

It is asleep, folded upon itself, eyelids and mouth sunk into forehead and cheek, an old man taking a nap. And it is not.

It is awake, a heraldic beast, crouched, to stare westward, alert for the Malverns, its eyes fixed upon Clee Hill and the Long Mynd, its nostrils dilated to sense far beyond into the hills of Wales. And it is not.

It is the Savages, their bones in the church at Elmley Castle, under the garish monuments, newly repainted, with inscriptions boasting of their family connections with the Duchess of Cumberland. And it is not.

It is archaeologists from Birmingham, bearded students and tweedy spinsters, digging in the earthworks near Overbury, excited by old bones, pottery fragments, tabulating, speculating, defining pit dwellings in the chalk. And it is not.

It is a young couple who had modernized an old cottage at Great Comberton, with a Van Gogh print in the living-room, and a three-year-old Morris Minor in the garage. And it is not.

It is the damp, dew dripping through the bracken, oozing slick upon clay and flint, soaking down into the meadows, and delicately settling in microscopic drops on the backs of the sheep between the twisted filaments of wool. And it is not.

It is an afternoon yet to come, a picnic with sandwiches and cider, the children running happy on the turf, with bees in the gorse, and a slight sunburn. And it is not.

And it is. The description is made. The attention becomes explicit. The hill has become familiar.

It has become a description, not a hill. But it declares a hill, a very particular hill, a remarkable hill: a hill which it is possible to know.

Miriam Waddington

FORTUNES

There is something in all of us
Pure and unconsumable;
After the forest fires
On the logged-over hillsides
You find the stubborn flowering
Of fireweed, or a green tree
Hung with a grab-bag of prophecies:
'You will live long, you will go on ocean voyages,
You will be lucky in love, or unlucky;
Beware the queen of spades; a handsome stranger
Will come into your life, the choices
Are dazzling.'

But whatever you do, whatever you choose,
It will end the same: we are not all lucky.
The stranger came and stayed a stranger,
We lived unhappily ever after,
The queen of spades dug my grave;
After the ten thousandth evening
Of dumb show and furious pantomime,
Fed up with Punch and Judy,
I went out in the autumn evening
To cry my anger to the stone-blind fields
Just as I was, untraditional, North American,
Jewish, Russian, and rootless in all four,
Religious and unaffiliated (uneasy in these also),
And held in a larger than life seize of hate.

It was then I felt my own purity,
I felt the young girl in me
Still like a green tree growing,
Tall and rooted, with the promise of flowering,

Whatever bastardy flower I could flower with now:
(A *Shloime Kapoir*, Solomon-upside-down flower,)
And why not? I always think of the Russian word
For soul, *dusha*, and the dusty Slavic village
Smelling so sweet with the grass uncut
And the white lilacs blooming—like a coming home
For my homeless half and half soul.

And I felt a kind of raised eyebrow yes-this-is-me,
This is no one else; not the laidly worm of Spindlestone,
No longer the bewitched princess,
But a wonderful living statue of marble stone
With her garments sculptured
Sailing against the wind of death.

John Wain

A SONG ABOUT MAJOR EATHERLEY

The book (Fernand Gigon's *Formula for Death—The Atom Bombs and After*) also describes how Major Claude R. Eatherley, pilot of the aircraft which carried the second bomb to Nagasaki, later started having nightmares. His wife is quoted as saying: 'He often jumps up in the middle of the night and screams out in an inhuman voice which makes me feel ill: "Release it, release it." '

Major Eatherley began to suffer brief periods of madness, says Gigon. The doctors diagnosed extreme nervous depression, and Eatherley was awarded a pension of 237 dollars a month.

This he appears to have regarded 'as a premium for murder, as a payment for what has been done to the two Japanese cities'. He never touched the money, and took to petty thievery, for which he was committed to Fort Worth prison.

(Report in *The Observer*, August 1958)

I

Good news. It seems he loved them after all.
His orders were to fry their bones to ash.
He carried up the bomb and let it fall.
And then his orders were to take the cash,

A hero's pension. But he let it lie.
It was in vain to ask him for the cause.
'Simply that if he touched it he would die.'
He fought his own, and not his country's wars.

His orders told him he was not a man:
An instrument, fine-tempered, clear of stain,
All fears and passions closed up like a fan:
No more volition than his aeroplane.

But now he fought to win his manhood back.
Steep from the sunset of his pain he flew
Against the darkness in that last attack.
It was for love he fought, to make that true.

II

To take life is always to die a little: to stop
any feeling and moving contrivance, however ugly,
unnecessary, or hateful, is to reduce by so much the total
of life there is. And that is to die a little.

To take the life of any enemy is to help him,
a little, towards destroying your own. Indeed, that is why
we hate our enemies: because they force us to kill them.
A murderer hides the dead man in the ground:
but his crime rears up and topples on to the living,
for it is they who now must hunt the murderer,
murder him, and hide him in the ground: it is they
who now feel the touch of death cold in their bones.

Animals hate death. A trapped fox will gnaw
through his own leg: it is so important to live
that he forgives himself the agony,
consenting, for life's sake, to the desperate teeth
grating through bone and pulp, the gasping yelps.

That is the reason the trapper hates the fox.
You think the trapper doesn't hate the fox?
But he does, and the fox can tell how much.
It is not the fox's teeth that grind his bones,
it is the trapper's. It is the trapper, there,
who keeps his head down, gnawing, hour after hour.

And the people the trapper works for, they are there too,
heads down beside the trap, gnawing away.

Why shouldn't they hate the fox? Their cheeks are smeared
with his rank blood, and on their tongues his bone
being splintered, feels uncomfortably sharp.
So once Major Eatherley hated the Japanese.

III

Hell is a furnace, so the wise men taught.
The punishment for sin is to be broiled.
A glowing coal for every sinful thought.

The heat of God's great furnace ate up sin,
Which whispered up in smoke or fell in ash:
So that each hour a new hour could begin.

So fire was holy, though it tortured souls,
The sinners' anguish never ceased, but still
Their sin was burnt from them by shining coals.

Hell fried the criminal but burnt the crime,
Purged where it punished, healed where it destroyed.
It was a stove that warmed the room of time.

No man begrudged the flames their appetite.
All were afraid of fire, yet none rebelled.
The wise men taught that hell was just and right.

The soul desires its necessary dread:
Only among the thorns can patience weave
A bower where the mind can make its bed.

Even the holy saints whose patient jaws
Chewed bitter rind and hands raised up the dead
Were chestnuts roasted at God's furnace doors.

The wise men passed. The clever men appeared.
They ruled that hell be called a pumpkin face.
They robbed the soul of what it justly feared.

Coal after coal the fires of hell went out.
Their heat no longer warmed the rooms of time,
Which glistened now with fluorescent doubt.

The chilly saints went striding up and down
To warm their blood with useful exercise.
They rolled like conkers through the draughty town.

Those emblematic flames sank down to rest:
But metaphysical fire can not go out.
Men ran from devils they had dispossessed,

And felt within their skulls the dancing heat
No longer stored in God's deep boiler-room.
Fire scorched their temples, frostbite chewed their feet.

That parasitic fire could race and climb
More swiftly than the stately flames of hell.
Its fuel gone, it licked the beams of time.

So time dried out and youngest hearts grew old.
The smoky minutes cracked and broke apart.
The world was roasting but the men were cold.

Now from this pain worse pain was brought to birth,
More hate, more anguish, till at last they cried,
'Release this fire to gnaw the crusty earth:

Make it a flame that's obvious to sight
And let us say we kindled it ourselves,
To split the skulls of men and let in light.

Since death is camped among us, wish him joy.
Invite him to our table and our games.
We cannot judge, but we can still destroy.'

And so the curtains of the mind were drawn.
Men conjured hell a first, a second time:
And Major Eatherley took off at dawn.

IV

Suppose a sea-bird,
its wings stuck down with oil, riding the waves
in no direction, under the storm-clouds, helpless,
lifted for an instant by each moving billow
to scan the meaningless horizon, helpless,
helpless, and the storms coming, and its wings dead,
its bird-nature dead:
      imagine this castaway,
loved, perhaps, by the Creator, and yet abandoned,
mocked by the flashing scales of the fish beneath it,
who leap, twist, dive, as free of the wide sea
as formerly the bird of the wide sky,
now helpless, starving, a prisoner of the surface,
unable to dive or rise:
      this is your emblem.

Take away the bird, let it be drowned
in the steep black waves of the storm, let it be broken
against rocks in the morning light, too faint to swim:
take away the bird, but keep the emblem.

It is the emblem of Major Eatherley,
who looked round quickly from the height of each wave,
but saw no land, only the rim of the sky,
into which he was not free to rise, or the silver
gleam of the mocking scales of the fish diving
where he was not free to dive.

Men have clung always to emblems,
to tokens of absolution from their sins.
Once it was the scapegoat driven out, bearing
its load of guilt under the empty sky
until its shape was lost, merged in the scrub.
Now we are civilized, there is no wild heath.
Instead of the nimble scapegoat running out
to be lost under the wild and empty sky,
the load of guilt is packed into prison walls,
and men file inward through the heavy doors.

But now that image, too, is obsolete.
The Major entering prison is no scapegoat.
His penitence will not take away our guilt,
nor sort with any consoling ritual:
this is penitence for its own sake, beautiful,
uncomprehending, inconsolable, unforeseen.
He is not in prison for his penitence:
it is no outrage to our law that he wakes
with cries of horror on his parching lips.
We do not punish him for cries or nightmares.
We punish him for stealing things from stores.

O, give his pension to the storekeepers,
Tell him it is the price of all our souls.
But do not trouble to unlock the door
and bring the Major out into the sun.
Leave him: it is all one: perhaps his nightmares
grow cooler in the twilight of the prison.
Leave him; if he is sleeping, come away.
But lay a folded paper by his head,
nothing official or embossed, a page
torn from your notebook, and the words in pencil.
Say nothing of love, of thanks, or penitence:
say only 'Eatherley, we have your message.'

Eugene Watters

SMITHSON'S GLIMPSE
OF THE THREE GRACES

(*Narrative Poem*)

'*Ille ego sum lignum qui non admittar in ullum*'
Ovid. Ep. ex Ponto, I.ii.35

Malahide, Saturday. Clouds come
Henna with heat. Salt and sun
Leave all flesh lazarous—
Tyrian tights and torsoed multitudes
Of leeches, baileys, baxters, smiths,
Recalled to the beaches out of bacon-shops,
From the drip and the stillness, dark destiny
Behind the blinds of education offices
And in the man's department, male and female,
The old and the middle-aged and their young with them,
Typists like graces coming together
From the Four Courts, the King's Inns,
Loosed and let go. Towels trailing,
Uncertain and half-naked go
The great mothers of mankind.
And we come late into the afternoon,
Called late into the afternoon,
From the rats and the vats and the cash-register,
From the surgical coat, the cold hams,
From the gold-hoards of grey buildings,
Travellers weary of world-markets
To look with strange eyes on continents
That do not seem to have endured too well
These fluctuations: what can we do
But gibe, gibber and adulterate
Tidal pools, trampling anemones?

Smithson barber, afternoon off,
Within the shadow of his wife stretched
Sizes it all up, a giant tattooed.
A black man beating a tom-tom
Chants from a booth in a dark tongue.
Flo calls for Freda, Freda
Euphrosyne . . . The names these girls . . . She knits.
Roll up, roll up. If you are out to see
Something interesting, something new—
But Smithson barber having seen it all
Drowses with one leg in the sun
Lazily like Italy on a warm day,
And while she knits his little waisted loves
Whose sad rumps are unhistoried look up
Out of his chest thickets. *Roll up, roll up.*
And the people talk through the long afternoon.

Their words tamper like black palms on the membrane,
His lids droop to in a trance of Christian-names,
The general murmur is pointed by the meticulous needles.
Calling, the drum throbs, calling
Come Flo, Come Freda,
Calling Euphrosyne, and now there is mention of
Diana, death, daughters, and ice-cream,
Married for nine months now, with lollipops,
Plasticisation and the new hair.
Their words weigh:
Dogs' names, names of deities,
Insinuation of voices, attitudes,
Cries and their offspring cry, the names
Float disjunct, throat constricts
Calling Freda for Christsake to hurry.
But their words are sundering words,
Expanding universes,
Until she is no more than a pimpernel in a place of stones,
And the son of the smith dreaming in deep water
Taken easily by the armpits listens
For the faint effrontery of the undistinguished shore,

Sizes it up and figures to himself.
That he is two miles from the edge of his century.

Rising and falling the tern cry,
Hover awhile arctic immigrants
Like windflowers above their archaic images.
The water has the barbarian hair of his chest,
His indigo ladies are disconsolate.
The birds dive, snow and joy commingling,
The wivery of the air, hardly the man's business.

Drowning is as lonely an experience as living.
A man must keep a thing or two to himself
When he encounters the bland and casual days,
The swingdoor ever in motion, a succession
Of sleekness, well-pointed, creased and bespectacled:
Life and death are cool customers surely.

Christ and Mary, isn't it a queer world
That sets him to barbering in this basement
Where it is difficult to keep body and soul together,
Sweeping the hair up in a slack moment,
Aware of himself out of conflicting mirrors
While a tap drips, hair slips and sidles
Middle-aged mostly, silver and brilliant
Lightly over the floorway; footsteps of people
Are passing above on the glass pavement,
Sound and shadow, ladies and gentlemen,
Sallowfooted, the sound soft as the shadow
And both felt, you'd think they had bare feet
Beating him to it, leaving him with the weight
Of the great labouring city to hold up
And bus after bus breaking in emerald.

Living and drowning, all one,
A naked bulb in a fogged air,
Or maybe the bulb is no more than a memory

In this rat-run of the universe where
We come to terms.

Come, come. But the dark drum
Is deliquescent, only the needle's tongue
Ticks time, pricks memory.
Flickering bayonets slant and present
Orderly succession of sharp light;
He is the gape on the marches of mankind,
Dislocated, idling in the gate, envying
What peace there was in the green drill of his time.
Fields of light tremble and are transposed,
Glass within glass to a great distance,
Face after face, the bleak and the passionate,
Neat as ninepence, like cards shuffled,
Mimic each other as the plane changes.
Hamsun is as hamsun does,
Bareheaded at doors to do business,
Tongue in cheek hanging about histories,
Bringing indelible lost loves
In thin ink (calling Euphrosyne)
Over the seas and the wet centuries,
Down to the round day's extremities,
Home with the trades to the five entries,
Whoring a little without much interest.
Come, come. But there is no drum
For drowned fingers, the phalanges are dumb
That drew the damned and quintessential myth,
Ungartering the girl and the stark smith
On the walls of palaces occupied for the moment,
On sagging canvases of temporary latrines
Where under the rain in a fit of abstraction
He has undone kingdoms as if they were buttons,
Saw the planes part, not without regret
For the sweet tooth that angered the god,
And he is fallen in a laxative sea,
A memory, a weed drifting without roots.
Generations go by shouldering death,

Time winks like cuts of a scissors,
He lies on the backbone and suspects a sky.
The medium is criss-crossed with dawn and evening,
Complex tranquillity;
Then gentle and simple the man's mind
Versed in exile breaks silence with itself:
I am he no timber will take in.

Here is the end as it was in the beginning,
Words' rhythm in a dark tongue
Conjuring the dreaming drowned irises.
Come. Come. Come.
Everything conspires to give a spring to the stone
And five minutes will make a difference
To the spirit and the earth lifting together—
Loose him, loose him, and let him go.
Malahide, Saturday. Tide slips,
The weed drips from rock-remnants
Of thunder and emerald into the new pools;
Ankle-deep comes Flo
Walking the thin-watered sands
In leaf of light, clear-footed,
Sharp drops blossom like periwinkles.
And naked laughter comes Euphrosyne
With sanguine nipples that are nub's neighbours
Redeeming all our littoral lost labours
An uttering in her throat's dusk quick
Nicknames for the unknowable, words' rut,
Phrases and cristophrase. And Freda comes.

Come. Come. Come.
The chief will show you how he can dance
On broken glass. Unperjured canvases
Bringing our trojan dead kindred
Home on our half-holidays. Smithson barber
Drowsing under the flicker and swarm
Sees all much as in Thorkill's time
When the sea was crude. Roll up, roll on,

Tom, tomb, typist and jungle-drum,
And the heart the ravens had now has its rhythm.
But Smithson dreams. *And if you are out to see*
Something interesting, something new,
This is the show. O quae regio?
This is the show you are looking for.
Smithson yawns up out of a great gurgle.
He will eat fire. O God, not again.
The sand burns, bears fellows
Screaming in clusters, black brethren,
And dance. The dirty man. Sees
Flo, Freda and Euphrosyne
Making their lips in his own century—
Ladies and gentlemen,
On broken bottles with his bare feet.

Buses tower, a line of them, lean to the kerb,
Window to window the light comes clean
Through upper decks abiding the next phase;
Birds rise to the lift of the wind changing,
The sun is on the western faces of the backsliding sea,
And words form in the charm of the returning crowds:
Fathers and daughters over the sand's ridges
With dogs leashed, clerks of the sessions
By sandpaths with selfheal and heartsease
Out of the hollows into the sun, leadbeaters,
Soldiers and seagraves, wine-merchants,
Over the short grass, you'd think they had bare feet,
Unordered procession and children running,
Browns and aubreys tilt into the light.
The women of the city enter taking their places,
And bus after bus numbered like the generations goes down,
Ordered and easy, gathering momentum
Until it is sound only, words' rhythm,
A local idiom in a dilation of awareness:

Goldsmiths and baileys, remarkable kindred.

Noël Welch

ADVENT

That Heaven should be hid is normal. Singular
Any part of me should for one instant
Be its hiding place. Yet for eight long months I've carried
Everything I see and things I shall never see
Because I carry Him. At first I scarcely

Dared to move, but a shell suffers the whole weight
Of the sea and the greenest pod is open
To the thrashing of the wind till the very moment
It is rent, so I trusting walked and grew
Heavier with Heaven at every step. I reach

From hill to hill, break out of rocks, enter
Flowers and trees and go fourfooted with the beasts
For, until He is strong enough to bear
His weak new state, I must bear with Him. But how
Shall I survive the hour Heaven looks up

At me without perhaps any recognition,
Demanding still only this hard faith
And the usual needs of a new-born child.
Already, the hands that run along this plank
Are not wholly mine nor are these feet that cross

And recross the floor. As often as I
Replace these dwindling candles with others
Tall and white, that cast before me their clean
Favouring shadows, I am myself renewed.
But I shall always link the sharp smell

Of fresh felled wood with this time of waiting
To cradle Him who cradles all the world,

That I already cradle privily
But must bring forth without strife or falsehood
Or one concession save those I make to His

Own unbelievable abiding self.
Meanwhile, I eat and sleep and sometimes laugh
At my own partridge shape nothing can now disguise
And at the cock's abrupt and dazzling cry
Weep for a nameless fear as women will.

G. P. Woodford

THE RULES OF ARTIFICE

The circle is that simple O
which seas and time bring pebbles to,
a trace of stars about the pole,
ripple, halo, iris, eye
and the sun's disc in the sky.

The plane, that categoric mean
to which the grain and crystal roll
and crumble torques of clay and stone
and mountains lean into the land
and hollow seas fill up with sand.

The line, a salient vertical,
artesian flame and waterspout,
sunlit cumulus and cliff,
raised from rivers horn and reed,
urgent penetrating seed.

Observe, conform, you conscious dust,
send through the rainbow a swift wheel,
establish floors before the last,
raise a mast among the reeds,
follow where an image leads.

AT PHAESTOS

The darkness swells the valley; night
Floods its large hollow with black air:
And into the oblivious slopes
Those pines relinquished by the light
Char and delete. A ruined floor

Which, looming, deader than the moon,
Sets a bleached angle, flag, and stair
Against a harmony of nothing
Opposes geometric lines
And, by opposing, best defines

The natural mystery it is in.
By daylight, earlier, lay below
An alive olive-bearing plain
Whose marching mountains paced the sky
With glittering epaulettes of snow—

The whole world was a horizon.
There water-green the orchards wound
To sunken contours, thick and still.
Or, ocean behind a hill,
Balanced a saucer of Aegean.

Easy to recognize those powers
Persistent in shining air
Whose heroic business is to live—
The abstract entities that declare
Themselves in language near to ours

And exist even if they grieve;
Lighthearted, mortal, and foredone,
The skeleton courtyards smiled at them:
Dead the successful city lay
Above its everliving meadows.

But shuttered in enormous gloom
That stuffs the valley at an hour
Which sees the landscape disappear,
Those courtyards, luminous and bare,
Tilt over a profound nothing;

The lightly transfixed stars appear,
And deities nailed to the sky
Wheel up in constellation—
Fading beyond the valley floor
A miles-off lantern says, a man.

THE CONTRIBUTORS

KINGSLEY AMIS was born in 1922, is married with two sons and a daughter. At present Lecturer in English at the University College of Swansea. Publications include: *Lucky Jim, That Uncertain Feeling, I Like It Here,* and *Take A Girl Like You* (novels); *A Case Of Samples* (verse); *New Maps Of Hell* (belles-lettres). (Page 15.)

ZOË BAILEY was born in 1930 and educated at Bishopshalt School, Hillingdon. She worked in the B.B.C. for ten years, during which time she obtained the University of London's Diploma in English Literature, studying at the City Literary Institute; following this, she was awarded a State Scholarship for Mature Students and is at present reading English Literature at New Hall, Cambridge. (Page 16.)

PATRICIA BEER was born in Devon in 1924. She worked for many years in Italy, and now teaches in London. Her first published collection of poems was *Loss Of The Magyar.* She will be, with Vernon Scannell and Ted Hughes, one of the three editors of *New Poems—1962.* (Page 18.)

THOMAS BLACKBURN was born in 1916, and is married with one daughter. He has published four collections of verse, including *In The Fire* and *The Next Word,* also a book of criticism, *The Price Of An Eye.* At present Lecturer in English at the College of S. Mark and S. John. Editor, with Kathleen Nott and C. Day Lewis, of *New Poems—1957.* (Page 20.)

JANET BURROWAY was born in 1936 in Arizona, where she attended state public school and spent one year at University, leaving for New York as 'guest editor' in the *Mademoiselle* Magazine College Board Contest; she spent three years at Barnard College, Columbia University, graduating cum laude in English Literature in 1958, and working part-time for the Poetry Center of Y.M.H.A., *The Paris Review,* and *The New Yorker.* She has just taken a First in English Literature at Cambridge, after two years there on a Marshall Aid Commemoration Commission Scholarship from the British Government. She spent the summer of 1959 working in Paris for the U.N. Children's

Fund. She attended the Yale School of Drama on the N.B.C.-C.B.S. Fellowship in 1961, and hopes to write for the theatre. Her poems and stories have appeared in *The Atlantic Monthly, Seventeen, Mademoiselle, New Poems by American Poets Number 2, Universities Poetry 2, Granta,* and *Delta,* and have been broadcast by the B.B.C. Her first novel, *Descend Again,* was published by Faber and Faber in 1960. (Page 21.)

CHARLES CAUSLEY was born in 1917 at Launceston, Cornwall, where he now writes and teaches. He is a Fellow of the Royal Society of Literature. His publications include *Farewell, Aggie Weston, Survivor's Leave,* and *Union Street* (poems); also *Hands To Dance* (short stories). He edited *Peninsula* (an anthology of West Country verse), and his new collection of verse, *Johnny Alleluia,* appeared in September, 1961. (Page 23.)

ALEX COMFORT was born in 1920 and educated at Highgate School, Trinity College, Cambridge, and London Hospital. He is a biologist, writer, and pacifist. He was co-editor of *Poetry Folios* and *New Road.* His publications include: *The Silver River, No Such Liberty, A Wreath For The Living, France And Other Poems, The Powerhouse, Letters From An Outpost,* etcetera. (Page 25.)

HILARY CORKE was born in 1921 at Malvern, Worcestershire, and educated at Charterhouse and Christ Church, Oxford. He was formerly Lecturer in Mediaeval English at the Universities of Cairo and Edinburgh, and is now a freelance writer. His first collection of verse, *The Early Drowned,* will be published this autumn. (Page 26.)

R. N. CURREY. Ralph Nixon Currey was born in Mafeking in 1907 and educated at Ermelo, Transvaal, at Kingswood School, Bath, and Wadham College, Oxford. Author of: *Tiresias, This Other Planet, Indian Landscape, Between Two Worlds* (poetry); *Formal Spring* (verse translations); *Poets Of The 1939-45 War* (Writers and Their Work pamphlet), etcetera. Edited, with R. V. Gibson, *Poems From India (Forces' Anthology).* Co-winner, with

Anthony Delius, of 1959 South African Poetry Competition. (Page 29.)

CLIFFORD DYMENT was born in 1914 in the Midlands, of Welsh parentage. He was educated at elementary schools and Loughborough Grammar School, and has worked as shop-assistant, travelling salesman, clerk, book reviewer, documentary film director. Since 1950 he has been a freelance writer and broadcaster. His books of poems include *Poems 1935–48* and *Experiences and Places*. 'The Desert' is one of a number of poems that had their origin in dreams, being written down immediately from the dream experience. Editor, with Roy Fuller and the late Montagu Slater, of the first P.E.N. Anthology, *New Poems—1952*. (Page 30.)

ANTHONY EDKINS was born in Cheshire in 1927 and educated at Cotton, Staffordshire. He worked in Madrid teaching English, on the Costa Brava as a travel courier, and in a San Francisco bookshop. At present lives in Hampstead and works in a travel agency. He is married to the American actress Maryellen Ray, and has two daughters. He has published translations from Spanish, travel articles, and one other poem. (Page 32.)

JULIAN ENNIS was born in 1915, read English at Oxford, and is now a Senior English Master in a boys' grammar school. He has edited numerous school textbooks, and his poems have appeared in various periodicals (some under a pen-name he has discontinued, Noel Scott); he has also written one-act plays for local performance, and is now engaged on writing a novel. (Page 34.)

D. J. ENRIGHT was born in 1920, and has taught English literature in Alexandria, Birmingham, Japan, Berlin, and Bangkok, and is at present Professor of English at the University of Malaya in Singapore. His publications include three novels, a book on Japan (*The World Of Dew*), a collection of critical essays, and three volumes of poetry, of which the most recent is *Some Men Are Brothers*. (Page 35.)

ROY FULLER was born in 1912. He has published six books of verse, of which the latest, *Brutus's Orchard*, received an Arts Council Prize in 1959; he is also a novelist, and his latest novel, *The Father's Comedy*, appeared in 1961. He is the solicitor to a large London Building Society and legal adviser to the Building Societies Association. Editor, with Clifford Dyment and the late Montagu Slater, of the first P.E.N. Anthology, *New Poems—1952*. (Page 36.)

KENNETH GEE was born in London in 1908; he is married, and lives in Surrey. His poems have appeared in many periodicals, and he has published *32 Poems* and *The Dead Can't Hurt You* (short stories). He is now painting as well as writing, and exhibited at the Woodstock Gallery in June 1961. (Page 37.)

ROBERT GITTINGS was born in 1911. After ten years at Cambridge as Scholar and Fellow of Jesus College, he has worked for the B.B.C. His publications, in verse, include *Wentworth Place, Famous Meeting*, and *The Makers Of Violence* (Canterbury Festival Play); in criticism and biography, *John Keats: The Living Year, The Mask Of Keats*, and *Shakespeare's Rival*. (Page 38.)

MICHAEL HAMBURGER was born in 1924 and educated at Westminster School, and Christ Church, Oxford. He has published several books of verse, the last of which is *The Dual Site*, and is now editing the poems and plays of Hofmannsthal. His new translation of poems by Hölderlin appeared in 1961. Editor, with Robert Conquest and Howard Sergeant, of *New Poems—1953*. (Page 40.)

CHRISTOPHER HAMPTON was born in London in 1929 and educated at Ardingly College, and Guildhall School of Music. He worked as a pianist and conductor before turning to literature. He has had poems published in *The Observer, T.L.S., Georgia Review, The Listener*, and broadcast on the B.B.C.

He has written articles on music and literature, and translated a novel by Guillot. His completed work includes four plays, an extended critical study, and a story for children. (Page 41.)

JOHN HEWITT was born in Belfast in 1907 and educated at Queen's University, Belfast. Since 1957 he has been Art Director of the Herbert Art Gallery and Museum, Coventry. He is an art critic and literary historian; in addition to writing a large quantity of verse, he has written short stories and a verse-play which has been broadcast. He is Poetry Editor of the Irish Quarterly, *Threshold*, and a member of the Irish Academy of Letters. His publications include: *Conacre, Compass, No Rebel Word, Those Swans Remember,* and *Ulster Poets: 1800–1850.* (Page 42.)

JOHN HOLLOWAY was born near London in 1920 and educated at Beckenham, and New College, Oxford; he was a Fellow of All Souls' College, 1946–60, and teaches English at Queens' College, Cambridge. His published books of verse are *The Minute* (1956) and *The Fugue* (1960). (Page 44.)

GRAHAM HOUGH was born in 1908 and educated at the University of Liverpool and Queens' College, Cambridge. His publications include: *The Last Romantics, The Romantic Poets, The Dark Sun, A Study Of D. H. Lawrence,* and *Image And Experience* (criticism), and *Legends and Pastorals* (poetry). (Page 45.)

TED HUGHES was born in 1930 in Mytholmroyd, West Yorkshire, and from Mexborough Grammar School he went to Pembroke College, Cambridge. He has published *The Hawk In The Rain* (1957) and *Lupercal* (1960). He, with Patricia Beer and Vernon Scannell, will edit *New Poems—1962.* (Pages 47 and 48.)

G. W. IRELAND was born in Douglas, Lanarkshire, Scotland, in 1927, and educated at Bathgate Academy and the Universities of Edinburgh, Caen, and Paris, with shorter periods at Harvard and Zürich. Since 1950 he has been Lecturer in French Language and Literature in the University of Leeds. His poetry has appeared in various periodicals as well as being broadcast by the Home Service and Third Programme of the B.B.C. The Third Programme has also broadcast a dramatic feature programme, *An Evening With Mallarmé,* and for two years he has been on the editorial board of *Poetry And Audience.* (Page 50.)

ADA JACKSON is married and lives in the Midlands, and has published six books of poetry: *The Widow, Narrow Homes, Against The Sun, World In Labour, In England Now,* and *Behold The Jew* (which won the Greenwood Prize in 1943, and has been issued in Braille). Her work has been broadcast frequently by the B.B.C. and N.B.C. (New York), and it has also appeared in about twelve anthologies. Her poetry has been translated into Spanish and Portuguese. (Page 52).

ELIZABETH JENNINGS was born in Lincolnshire in 1926 and educated at Oxford University. She has published four books of poems, the first of which won an Arts Council Prize and the second the Somerset Maugham Award for 1956. She has recently published a book for children about poetry, and completed a study of the relations between mystical experience and the making of poems entitled *Every Changing Shape.* She has just finished nearly two years as reader to a London publisher, and is now devoting her time to her own writing; she has completed a fourth book of poems, written a pamphlet about contemporary poetry (for the British Council), edited an anthology and made a translation of Michelangelo's sonnets. She, with Dannie Abse and Stephen Spender, edited *New Poems—1956.* (Pages 54 and 55.)

GLYN JONES was born in Merthyr Tydfil, Wales, in 1905. He is the author of *The Blue Bed* and *The Water Music* (short stories); *Poems* and *The Dream Of Jake Hopkins* (verse); *The Valley, The City, The Village,* and *The Learning Lark* (novels); also, with Dr. T. J. Morgan, *The Saga Of Llywarch The Old* (Golden Cockerel Press), a translation and reconstruction of some ancient Welsh poems. (Page 56.)

RICHARD KELL was born in County Cork, Ireland, in 1927, and educated in South India, Belfast, and Dublin, and graduated from Trinity College, Dublin. He now teaches in London. In addition to his poems (many of which have been broadcast and published) he has written some short stories and essays. At present he is working on a novel, and his first book of poems will be published by Chatto and Windus in 1962. (Page 57.)

FRANCIS KING was born in 1923 and educated at Shrewsbury and Balliol College, Oxford. He worked for the British Council in Italy, Greece, Egypt, Finland, and now does so in Japan. He has published eight novels, including *The Dividing Stream* and *The Widow*; a volume of short stories, *So Hurt And Humiliated*, and a collection of poems, *Rod of Incantation*. His new novel, *The Custom House*, was published in September, 1961. (Page 58.)

THOMAS KINSELLA was born in Dublin in 1928, and works in Government service. His publications include *The Sons Of Usnech* and other translations from the early Irish; *Poems* (1956), *Another September* (1958), *Moralities* (1960); all published by The Dolmen Press, Dublin. (Page 59.)

JAMES KIRKUP was born in 1912. He was Professor of English, Tohoku University, Japan, 1959–61. He has published seven volumes of poetry, the latest being *The Prodigal Son*, and two volumes of autobiography. His most recent works are *These Horned Islands: A Journal Of Japan*, and a novel, *Births, Marriages And Deaths*. He has also done many translations, and radio and television scripts, including *The True Mistery Of The Passion* which was televised from Bristol Cathedral, Easter 1960. He was the first holder of the Gregory Fellowship in Poetry at Leeds University. (Page 61.)

PHILIP LARKIN was born in 1922, and has published *A Girl In Winter* (novel) and *The North Ship* and *The Less Deceived* (poems). He is Librarian to the University of Hull and, with Bonamy Dobrée and Louis MacNeice, edited *New Poems—1958*. (Page 63.)

MICHAEL LEVIEN was born in India in 1927 and educated at Harrow; he served three years in the Army. He has travelled in the Far East, and lived for a time in Italy. He has published poems in *The London Magazine* and in *Two Cities*, and was joint-editor of an anthology of prose and poetry, *Springtime Three*, which came out in the spring of 1961. (Page 64.)

EDWARD LUCIE-SMITH was born in Kingston, Jamaica, in 1933, and educated at King's School, Canterbury, and Merton College, Oxford. He is now living in Chelsea, and works in advertising and as an art critic. (Page 65.)

GEORGE MacBETH was born in Scotland in 1932 and educated at King Edward VII School, Sheffield, and New College, Oxford. He now works as a Talks Producer for the B.B.C. Third Programme, and has published one book of poems, *A Form Of Words* (Fantasy Press, 1954). (Page 66.)

ROY MACNAB was born in Durban, South Africa, in 1923, and educated in Natal, and Oxford University. He is Cultural Attaché to the South African Embassy in Paris. His published poetry includes: *Testament Of A South African* and *The Man Of Grass*, and his work has appeared in the following anthologies: *Oxford Poetry 1947, South African Poetry, Towards The Sun*, and *Poets In South Africa*. (Page 68.)

LOUIS MacNEICE was born in 1907 and educated at Marlborough and Merton College, Oxford. Since 1941 he has been a Feature Writer and Producer for the B.B.C. His publications include *Collected Poems, Autumn Sequel, Visitations* and *Solstices*. (Page 70.)

ADRIAN MITCHELL was born in 1932 and educated at Dauntsey's School and Christ Church, Oxford. He has been a reporter on the *Oxford Mail* and the *Evening Standard*. In May 1960 he quit newspapers to work alone, and in four months completed a novel, *If You See Me Comin'*, a collection of poems, *Veteran With A Head Wound*, and a TV play, *Animals Can't Laugh*. (Page 72.)

EDWIN MORGAN was born in Glasgow in 1920, and is Lecturer in English at Glasgow University. His publications include *Beowulf* (verse translation), *The Cape Of Good Hope* (long poem), *Poems From Eugenio Montale* (verse translations), and *Sovpoems* (translations from Russian). His poems have appeared in the following anthologies: *The Golden Horizon, Springtime, Lyric Poetry Of The Italian Renaissance, New Poems—1954* and *New Poems—1955,* and *Honour'd Shade.* (Page 73.)

BETTY PARVIN was born in 1917. She left convent school, Catholicism, and Cardiff seventeen years later, married a Nottingham solicitor and has one son. Her poems and stories have been broadcast and have appeared in various magazines and reviews. (Page 79.)

WILLIAM PLOMER (D.Litt.) was born in 1903, and his early life was divided between England, South Africa, and Japan. He served with the Naval Intelligence Division, 1940–5. His *Collected Poems* (1960) were taken from seven earlier books, and he has also published fiction, biographies, and autobiographies. He edited *Kilvert's Diary* (three volumes: 1938–40), and was the librettist of Benjamin Britten's three-act opera, *Gloriana* (1953). (Page 80.)

JONATHAN PRICE was born in 1931 and educated at Kingswood School, Bath, and Lincoln College, Oxford. His poem have been published in the *Fantasy Poets* series and various magazines and anthologies. He works as a London publisher's editor, is an associate editor of *The Transatlantic Review,* and occasionally broadcasts on poetry programmes. (Page 82.)

PETER REDGROVE was born in 1932, and has published *The Collector And Other Poems.* 'Disguise' is from his second book of verse, *The Nature Of Cold Weather,* which is now in preparation. (Page 83.)

JAMES REEVES was born in London in 1909, and educated at Stowe and Jesus College, Cambridge. He has published a number of books for children and four for adults—these appeared in 1960 as *Collected Poems 1929–59*. He has also edited two books of traditional English verse from the Mss. of the folk-song collectors of fifty years ago—*The Idiom Of The People* and *The Everlasting Circle*. (Page 85.)

VERNON SCANNELL was born in 1922. His publications include *A Mortal Pitch* and *The Masks Of Love* (poetry) and *The Fight* (prose). He has also published a thriller, *The Shadowed Place*. He, with Patricia Beer and Ted Hughes, will edit *New Poems—1962*. (Pages 86 and 88.)

E. J. SCOVELL was born in Sheffield in 1907, and educated at Carsterton School, Westmorland, and Somerville College, Oxford. She is married to a biologist and has two children, and lives in Oxford. Her publications are *Shadows Of Chrysanthemums, The Midsummer Meadow* and *The River Steamer*. (Page 90.)

STEVIE SMITH was born in Hull, and has worked in a publisher's office. Her publications include *Novel On Yellow Paper, Over The Frontier,* and *The Holiday* (novels); *A Good Time Was Had By All, Tender Only To One, Mother, What Is Man? Harold's Leap, Not Waving But Drowning,* and *Selected Poems* (poems and drawings); also *Some Are More Human Than Others* (sketch book). (Page 91.)

MARGARET STANLEY-WRENCH was born in 1916 and educated at Channing School, Highgate, and Somerville College, Oxford. In 1937 she won the Newdigate Prize. Her publications include *Newsreel And Other Poems, The Splendid Burden* (verse play), *A Tale For The Fall Of The Year* (poems). She has also written children's books and scripts for the B.B.C. Schools Programme, and has had several long narrative and dramatic poems broadcast in the Third Programme. Her biography of St. Thomas More for young people is to be published shortly. (Page 94.)

HAL SUMMERS was born in Yorkshire in 1911 and educated in Edinburgh and Oxford. He now works in Whitehall and lives in Kent. His publications include *Smoke After Flame*, *Hinterland* and *Poems In Pamphlet*. (Page 95.)

DONALD THOMAS was born in 1934 and educated at Queen's College, Taunton, and Balliol College, Oxford. He has contributed poems to the B.B.C. Third Programme, *The Listener*, *The Times Literary Supplement*, *Outposts*, *Gemini*, etcetera. (Page 96.)

R. S. THOMAS was born in 1913. He lives in Wales. His publications include *Song At The Year's Turning* (1955) and *Poetry For Supper* (1958). (Page 97.)

ANTHONY THWAITE was born in 1930 and educated at Kingswood School and Christ Church, Oxford. From 1955 to 1957 he lectured in English Literature at the University of Tokyo, and since then he has been with the B.B.C. in London as a producer in the Features Department (Sound). His publications are *Home Truths* (1957, poetry) and *Contemporary English Poetry—An Introduction* (1959, criticism). He is joint-editor with Geoffrey Bownas of a forthcoming *Penguin Book Of Japanese Verse*. (Page 98.)

SYDNEY TREMAYNE was born in Ayr in 1912, and went to school at Ayr Academy. He then became a journalist and worked for newspapers in many parts of the country, and on national newspapers in London (with an interlude as a fireman) for twenty-four years. He now lives in Kent, and has published three books of verse so far, *Time And The Wind*, *The Hardest Freedom* and *The Rock And The Bird*. (Page 99.)

GAEL TURNBULL was born in Edinburgh in 1928 and educated at Cambridge and in Canada and the United States. He is at present living in California. He has published poems in a number of magazines and recently edited *Migrant*. (Page 100.)

MIRIAM WADDINGTON was born in Winnipeg at the end of the first world war, and has since lived in Montreal and Toronto. She has been married, and has two sons, and is a graduate of the University of Toronto and the University of Pennsylvania School of Social Work. She is a social caseworker by profession, and secretary of the Canadian P.E.N. Centre. She has published three books of poetry, the most recent being *The Season's Lovers* (Ryerson, Toronto, 1958), and her work has appeared in Canadian, British, and American periodicals and most Canadian verse anthologies, including *The Oxford Book Of Canadian Verse*. (Page 102.)

JOHN WAIN was born in 1925 and educated at the High School, Newcastle-under-Lyme, and St. John's College, Oxford; Fereday Fellow, St. John's College, 1946–9, and Lecturer in English Literature at the University of Reading from 1947 to 1955, when he resigned to become a freelance author and critic. His publications include *Hurry On Down, Living In The Present, The Contenders, A Travelling Woman* (novels); *Nuncle And Other Stories* (short stories); *Preliminary Essays* (criticism); and *A Word Carved On A Sill* and *Weep Before God* (poetry). (Page 104.)

EUGENE WATTERS was born in Ballinasloe, Co. Galway, in 1919, and is Gaelic scriptwriter at the Abbey Theatre, Dublin, Oireachtas Prizewinner in Gaelic poetry, and a contributor to all the Gaelic magazines and anthologies. He won the Arts Council (Ireland) Award for verse-tragedy in 1959. He contributes reviews to *The Tablet*, and articles to *The Catholic Gazette* and *Time and Tide,* and poems to *Bell, Envoy,* and *The Irish Times.* (Page 110.)

NOËL WELCH was born in London and educated at Parsons Mead, Ashstead, and St. Hilda's College, Oxford. She has travelled a good deal in Africa, France, and Spain, and now lives on Dartmoor, and apart from short spells abroad hopes to stay there for ever. Publication, *Ten Poems*. (Page 116.)

G. P. WOODFORD was born in 1915 and educated at Kingswood School and New College, Oxford. By profession he is a civil servant, formerly in India and now at home. He lives in Hampstead. He has published various articles on town planning. (Page 118.)

DAVID WRIGHT was born in Johannesburg in 1920 and educated at Northampton School for the Deaf and Oriel College, Oxford. His publications include *Poems, Moral Stories, Monologue Of A Deaf Man,* and a prose translation of *Beowulf.* He is the editor of *X,* the quarterly magazine of literature and art, and edited *The Faber Book Of Twentieth Century Verse.* He is married, and lives in London. (Page 119.)